4/09

Selected Translations
W. D. Snodgrass

SELECTED TRANSLATIONS

W. D. Snodgrass

BOA Editions, Ltd. ❧ Rochester, NY ❧ 1998

LC #: 97–74818
ISBN: 1–880238–60–8

First Edition
98 99 00 01   7 6 5 4 3 2 1

Publications by BOA Editions, Ltd.—
a not-for-profit corporation under section 501 (c) (3)
of the United States Internal Revenue Code—
are made possible with the assistance of grants from
the Literature Program of the New York State Council on the Arts,
the Literature Program of the National Endowment for the Arts,
the Lannan Foundation, the Sonia Raiziss Giop Charitable Foundation,
the Eric Mathieu King Fund of The Academy of American Poets,
as well as from the Mary S. Mulligan Charitable Trust,
the County of Monroe, NY,
and from many individual supporters.

Cover Design: Daphne Poulin-Stofer
Cover Art: "W.D. Chasing Fireflies" by DeLoss McGraw,
Courtesy of the Collection of Stéphane Janssen, AZ.
Author Drawing by Marin Sorescu
Typesetting: Richard Foerster
Printed in the United States by McNaughton & Gunn
BOA Logo: Mirko

BOA Editions, Ltd.
Alexandra Northrop, Chair
A. Poulin, Jr., President & Founder (1976–1996)
260 East Avenue
Rochester, NY 14604

for Kathy
in every language

CONTENTS

II. FOLK SONGS AND BALLADS

III. ART SONGS

PREFACE

Once, when I was a student at the University of Iowa, I stumbled onto a translation which was just plain wrong—a version of one of Rilke's *Sonnets to Orpheus* that asserted the blunt opposite of what Rilke had said. This version told young poets to sing out their longings; Rilke had said the *real* song was not about desire, but about praise for what *is*. Yet this "translation" appeared in a respected publication; the translator was well known, had recently read his poems there at Iowa. Maybe I *could* translate a poem, after all—even *that* poem. I certainly couldn't do worse.

Later I ran into Robert Lowell who said, as nearly as I can recall, "Sometimes your own work gets so painful you have to set it aside for a while. At those times, try some translations—you don't have to know the language. Take one of Mrs. Norton's prose versions of Rilke, for instance, and kick it around to see if you can make an English poem out of it. That at least keeps your hand in."

As it turned out, there were usually both poems *and* translations I had set aside, like plants in a window box, going back every so often to see if anything had come up. In time, I made translations of songs and poems from nearly twenty languages and dialects—none of which I could read or speak. Strangely enough, there are no translations here from the one language, ancient Greek, I had learned to read with any fluency. The translations here were all done from a prose pony (or preferably several prose ponies to break down habits of phrasing) or with scholars and friends native to the original language. This provides a wonderful relief from hours of isolation at your desk, as well as from your own narrow selection of thoughts and phrasings.

I have remarked elsewhere (half joking, but *only* half) that it's easier to translate poems from a language you don't know. My problems usually have *not* been like those with the Rilke sonnet mentioned above—not of getting the dictionary sense, of singing the right notes, but rather of recreating a sufficient harmonization and orchestration in English. Bilingual translators face a difficulty: having translated a poem, they cannot read their own version without hearing, simultaneously, the original still stored elsewhere in the brain. This offers a compounded experience—to *them*. Alas, translations aren't made for the bilingual. Though translating a poem should teach you much about its original—its textures, sound effects, formal workings, language and image constructions—you will almost never be able to recreate the same effects in another language. And you can waste years trying. Meantime, you may overlook the new language's possibilities. Transcribing the mere tune without drawing on your new orchestra's range of instruments, harmony and tone color, you deprive your audience of that rich complex of meaning and feeling we bargain for in a poem.

Still, though my purposes have demanded certain liberties, I have usually stayed quite close to the dictionary sense of the original. I have seldom departed from the denotative sense as, for instance, Lowell did in his "imitations." I have no theoretical objection to such departures—if we allow Thomas Wyatt his liberties in rendering Petrarch, why forbid them to Lowell? For myself, though, I have kept the literal sense whenever I could—after all, the breadth and variety of the English language gives you an incredible range of possibilities inside the limits of a so-called literality.

There *were* times, especially in songs, when I couldn't keep the dictionary sense. I have done much work with specialists in early music and admire their dedication to authenticity. But, if I may hazard another paradox, it's sometimes more authentic to render a song in the audience's language than in the original. The texts of many songs, after all, were *meant* to be heard and grasped. To deliver Oswald von Wolkenstein's "Das Fuegt Sich . . ." ("There Came a Time") in even the best Bavarian accent cannot convey to a present-day audience this delightful scoundrel's yarn about his life as a soldier and layabout all over Europe. Similarly, "Da le si le das" ("Do It So It's Done") from the *Cancionero Musical de Palacio* (*Palace Songbook*) is full of sexual innuendo about girls from Carasa and Logroño—villages which may not even exist today. I've substituted West Virginia and Carolina: the first because of an old scurrilous joke that a West Virginia virgin was a six-year-old who could outrun her father and brothers. I scarcely know a girl from Carolina; I only know what the name rhymes with. Without the sly jokes, the obvious but unspoken rhymes, the song has no reason to exist. The result, of course, is politically incorrect. Palace-dwellers seldom worried about that.

As noted above, I've done translations from a wide variety of languages; costs limit the extent of one's selection. Lore Segal and I did roughly 150 of Christian Morgenstern's poems; only seven appear in this volume. There are no examples from the famous "Gay Graveyard" in Transylvania; without photographs of the colorful and sometimes comic grave markers, the obituary verses would lose much of their point.

Similarly, it does not make sense to give too wide a sampling of songs unless music can be included. Stylistically, song texts are often less interesting, less dense in texture than other poetic texts; the complication of melody is yet to be added. To make singable versions, one must often give up otherwise excellent phrasings which will not sing well. I have made versions for seven songs by Bernart de Ventadorn, the most famous Troubadour of his time, but only one is given here. Elsewhere, I have omitted stanzas from some of the songs.

The translations included here are divided into three sections: poems, folk songs or ballads, and art songs. The translations of poems usually come from either very early or very late in my career. In mid-career I translated only songs, since many fine American poets were translating poems while my background in music might make this area more accessible to me. Besides, I simply wanted to sing these songs myself and was unable to learn or to pronounce acceptably the original languages. Some of these translations have been performed live or else recorded by such early music groups as the Columbia Collegium or the Waverley Consort and by individual singers and lutenists. As noted above, expense forbids reprinting my transcriptions of the music; other transcriptions are available, however, in standard sources.

The discrimination between folk and art songs should be clear. Folk songs denote pieces of unknown amateur authorship, composed by and for a peasant or folk community; both text and melody may exist in many versions within that society. Obviously, some particularly gifted singer or collector may have radically influenced our recognition of a song; from my point of view, this is no corruption. By the term ballad, here, I refer to a special category of folk song, recognized as more meaningful, widespread, and resonantly tragic or comic. Art songs, on the other hand, were usually created by a professional musician/composer; we take this composer's version alone to be authentic. Such pieces were usually made for a courtly or a cultivated middle- or upper-class audience.

These translations intend to satisfy as English-language poems or songs. We all recognize that literal translation is impossible. That actually makes it a little less daunting as a task: when you fail—as you often will—at least you needn't feel ashamed of timidity or slack ambition. If you're going to lose a fight, better lose it to a large opponent; even to win against a smaller man involves some disgrace—besides, if he wins, a small man's more likely to kill you.

I.
POEMS

Ovid

EUROPA

Brave in brocades, the ladies come flouncing
   Through ferns opening toward the salt banks
Gathering flowers and half dancing
   Their games and the gay girls' pranks

That still stay formal as their finery
   Of tidal gowns. Whiter than gulls,
Their bare arms toss above the greenery
   Where doze the strayed and browsing bulls—

Beasts of her father's sovereign farms,
   Gone prodigal. With what keen shrieks,
With laughter, and what thrashing arms,
   They drive those great louts down the beach

To herd them home. Yet, once on shore,
   The frivolous ladies hush and frolic
Halts. Something unseen before
   Among these herds—a ghost white bullock.

Say that his chest is like a swan's
   Soft contours. Like cut crystal
Or like fluted candles, his two horns.
   He's noways harsh, crude, or bestial

But moves above the waddling herd
   As gracefully as her lamb sandal.
Passing, swings his anvil head
   Toward her and lows. His eyes are gentle.

Giddy ladies could never suspect
   Divinity among such beasts;
But trail flowers down his dewlapped neck
   As for a sacrifice or feast

Ovid

Of marriage, for a funeral
  Or rites of blood to the newborn;
They heap their flowers on the animal,
  Looping them thick around his horns.

She brings armfuls of blooming plants
  For fodder, and combs his kinky forelocks.
He fawns, licking her wrists and hands
  Then stops. And rolls about the burdock

Or kneels there on the sun-warm sands
  Letting her smooth his creamy sides;
Slow muscles roll beneath her hand
  As to the keel rolls the full tide.

It is the lady who grows bolder.
  Familiar with his games and pranks
She mounts his prostrate bulge of shoulder
  And takes her seat upon his bristled flank

Draped in their bright undamaged garlands.
  Her ladies murmur against such nerve.
She guides him on the giving sands
  And through the shallow spuming surf.

At first he wades just to the fetlock
  And back. Then plods along the shore.
Next, splashing in combers to his hocks
  And back. And each time more and more

He carries her out to a drowning depth
  Of sea, plunging toward the channel
Where to leave him is her death.
  Her right hand grips one horn like a gunwale

Or chariot railing where she rides
  In mortal triumph stiff with dread
Astride the brawny god. A wide
  Wallowing sea is all ahead.

Her maids faint or pull their hair
  Shrieking after their lord's daughter.
No human voice shall reach her ear
  In all that bellowing of deep waters

But still she looks back to her friends
  And home. Salt bites her face and her hair
Is drenched in ocean without end.
  Her garments part in the weathering air.

Antonio Vivaldi (?)

THE FOUR SEASONS

I. SPRING

Springtime has come around again; now merrily
  Small birds salute the season as they sing;
  Calm zephyrs sigh across the waters airily
  Which answer back in their sweet murmuring.
Soon, though, the sky is cloaked with robes of black;
  Thunder and lightning come—the spring's loud heralds.
  Yet once the storm subsides and calm comes back
  The birds, just as before, take up their carols.
Where the green meadow flowers all around,
  Among soft whisperings of leaves and plants
  The goatherd sleeps next to his faithful hound.
Now shepherds' bagpipes start the reveling;
  Under clear skies the nymphs and shepherds dance
  Decked out in the full radiance of the spring.

II. SUMMER

In the fierce season, scorched dry by the sun,
  Men languish, beasts languish, the pine trees singe;
  The cuckoo lifts his clear voice, one by one
  Joined by the turtledove and the goldfinch.
Zephyr gently blows, but then suddenly
  Boreas rushes in, roughly contending.
  The shepherd boy weeps with anxiety
  As to his fate and the wild storm impending.
Deprived of rest, worn out, his limbs grow weary;
  He fears the lightning's flashing, the loud thunder,
  And all the wasps and flies, swarming with fury.
Too soon it comes true, everything he dreads:
  The skies rumble and flash; tree trunks break under
  Lightning blasts; hail cuts off the ripe wheat's heads.

III. AUTUMN

With songs and dances, peasants celebrate
  A teeming harvest time. They drink so deep
  Of Bacchus' liquors that, inebriate,
  They end their joys sunk into heavy sleep.
Soon now the dancing and the song are done;
  This season with its gentle, pleasant air
  Seems to invite us, each and every one,
  To the delights of slumber, free from care.
The hunters set out at the break of day
  Joining the chase with muskets, horns and hounds;
  The beast takes flight, but they track, still, their prey.
Bewildered, worn out with the fearful sounds
  Of dogs and muskets, wounds that terrify,
  Borne down, exhausted, finally it must die.

IV. WINTER

To shiver, stiff with cold, in glittering snow
  Under the breath of chill winds, roughly battering;
  To rush, stamping with both feet as you go
  In tyrannous cold that keeps a man's teeth chattering;
To spend contented days by the fireside
  While, outside, rain streams down bedrenching all;
  To walk on the ice, but with a slow stride
  Cautiously, fearful that you might fall;
Step boldly out then, slip, fall to the ground
  But then run vigorously on once more
  Till the ice breaks, dissolving all around;
To hear, issuing through iron gates, the noise
  Of Boreas, Sirocco, the winds at war—
  This, then, is winter; it, too, has its joys.

Joseph Freiherr von Eichendorff

ON MY CHILD'S DEATH

Clocks strike in the distance,
Already the night grows late,
How dimly the lamp glistens;
Your bed is all made.

It is the wind goes, only,
Grieving around the house;
Where, inside, we sit lonely
Often listening out.

It is as if, how lightly,
You must be going to knock,
Had missed your way and might be
Tired, now, coming back.

We are poor, poor stupid folk!
It's we, still lost in dread,
Who wander in the dark—
You've long since found your bed.

Gerard de Nerval

EL DESDICHADO

I am the shadowed, the widowed, the disconsolate,
The Prince of Aquitania whose tower is abolished;
My single star is dead—my constellated lute
Bears only the black sun from "Melancholy."

You that, in my night of tombs, brought consolation,
Give me Posilipo, the Italian sea, again;
The flower that comforted my heart in desolation,
The trellis where the roses marry to the vine.

Am I Amor or Phoebus . . . Lusignan or Biron?
On my forehead, still, the queen's kiss holds its fire.
I've dreamed within the grotto of the swimming siren;

I have crossed over Acheron, triumphant, twice
And modulated, one by one, on Orpheus' lyre
Sighs of the saints and the damned spirits' cries.

"Koz'ma Petrovich Prutkov"

JUNKER SCHMIDT

The leaf wilts. Summer slowly drains out.
Frost lies white as crystal.
Junker Schmidt, with a pistol,
Wants to blow his brains out.

Wait, wait, you giddy madman! Learn:
Greenery is no goner.
Junker Schmidt, my word of honor,
Summer will return.

—translated with Tanya Tolstoy

REMEMBRANCE OF THINGS PAST:
Heine-esque

Forty years will soon have passed
Since I first knew you as a maiden
With your little rumpled apron
And your corset laced up fast.

You felt uncomfy, bound in it,
And said for me alone to hear,
"Unlace my corset in the rear;
I just can't run around in it."

Full of anxiety, overwrought,
I got your corset all untied.
Giggling, you ran off to hide.
I, though, stood fixed in solemn thought.

—translated with Tanya Tolstoy

THE DEACONESS AND THE WORM: A Fable

A worm, once, on a Deaconess's neck, began to crawl and squirm.
  Whereupon, she bade her butler to fetch out the serpent.
Whereupon, the Deaconess got pawed over by her servant.
  "But what are you doing, wretch?" "Madame, squashing the worm."

Now should a worm crawl on thy neck, O Reader, look thou to it:
Squash him thyself; don't let the butler do it.

—translated with Tanya Tolstoy

LOVE OF HONOR

Give me brains like Socrates,
Aspasia's fancies, fertile,
The tub of Diogenes,
Also Venus's girdle.
Give me Psyche's step, so light,
And Cicero's rhetoric,
Zeus's splendor and might,
Also his magic stick.

Give me Sappho's girlish tongue,
The rage of Juvenal.
Give me Cleonas's lung
That deafened the whole forum,
Samson's power and fury,
The sword of Hannibal
Which for old Carthage's glory
Lopped men's heads off for 'em.

Give me Virgilius's song,
Seneca's skull of bone—
The wordings of my tongue

"Koz'ma Petrovich Prutkov"

Would tremble mankind with tone.
With courage of Lycurgus,
Circumspecting around,
I would shake all Petersburg as
My verses should resound.

Note, now, a second sense:
From oblivion's dark miasma
I should save my good name, hence:
Prutkov . . . the loud name Koz'ma.

—translated with Tanya Tolstoy

Mihai Eminescu

STAR

It's been a long way for that bright
   Star, new-risen in the skies;
Thousands of years passed while its light
   Came traveling to our eyes.

Long since, it's burned itself away
   Perhaps, out in the blue of space;
Only just now, though, that ray
   Ignites here in our gaze.

The icon of that dead star climbs
   Slowly into the heavens where
We couldn't see it at the time—
   We do, now it's not there.

So is it, utterly, when desire
   Dies out in the depths of night:
Our own love's extinguished fire
   Follows us still with light.

—translated with Ioan and Kitty Popa,
Sever Trifu, and Neli Ament

SONNETS (I)

Autumn of the year outside, the leaves scattered,
The wind hurls heavy drops against the pane;
You take, from their worn envelopes, old letters
And in an hour thumb through your life again.

Wasting time on sweet nothings, airy matters,
You'd not want anyone knocking at your door;
Or while the sleet falls outside, even better
To sit by the fire drowsing off more and more.

So in my armchair, pensive, I stare at nothing,
Dreaming about the fairy Dochia's story;
Rank on rank, thick mists around me rise.

And I hear then, suddenly, a dress rustling,
A soft footfall barely brushing the floor
And slender, cold hands covering my eyes.

—translated with Dona Roşu and Luciana Costea

ONE WISH LEFT

Just one wish left: that I might
   be allowed to die
in the quiet twilight
   with the sea nearby;
that gentle be my sleep,
   the old forest nigh,
over the serene, deep
   waters, a clear sky;
no need for a rich coffin
   or streaming banners; I
would have the bed be woven
   of young boughs where I lie.

Let no one speak of grief
   or shed tears at my mound
but through the withered leaf
   let Fall resound;
let springs their fresh streams drop
   still murmuring to the ground,

the moon above the fir tree's top
    glide on her round;
may sheepbells mingle
    with cool nightwind's sound,
the holy lime tree sprinkle
    its twigs and branches down.

I shall no longer be
    the vagrant I've been;
memories will, lovingly,
    drift to snow me in,
and evening stars again
    that over dark firs shone
will smile as on a friend
    warmly and well known;
the sea's rough tongue may cry
    its endless bitter tone,
but I'll be dust and I
    will be alone.

—translated with Dona Roşu and Luciana Costea

NOW THE SONGBIRDS, ALL ADROWSE

Now the songbirds, all adrowse,
  Come together out of sight
In their nests among the boughs;
    So; good night.

Only the small streams go on weeping
  While the dark woods hush and cease.
Even the garden flowers are sleeping;
    Sleep, then, in peace.

Mihai Eminescu

Across the water, the swan's gliding
   Toward the reeds that hide its nest;
Angels 'round you still abiding,
    Calm be your rest.

Now, over night's broad elfery,
   The ancient, proud moon claims her height.
All is peace, all harmony;
    Now, good night.

—translated with Augustin Maissen

Arthur Rimbaud

MEMORY

I

Clear waters; like the salt in teardrops of a child,
The white of women's flesh assaulting the sun's light;
The silks of pennons, massed, and as lilies undefiled,
Under walls some Maid held once, their defending knight.

Games of the angels . . . No—this gold stream on its march
Stirs black arms, heavy, chill above all, through grass. She,
Who's gloomy, with blue sky for her bed's blue canopy,
Draws curtains—shadows of the hills and of the arch.

II

Ha! Clear bouillon spreads out, shimmering over the rocks.
This water now furnishes for its waiting beds
A bottomless, pale gold. Girls' green and faded frocks
Are willow trees outbursting with unbridled birds.

Golden as a *louis*, the warm and pure lid of an eye,
This Kingcup, just at prompt noon, from its tarnished mirror
Turns, jealous—your marriage faith, O Spouse!—to the sky
Gone gray in its own heat: the dear and rosebright sphere.

III

Too upright, Madame in the nearby meadow lingers
Where Man-of-the-Earth's a snowdrift. Sunshade clamped
             in fingers,
She tramps the flower clusters—proud, too proud indeed—
Her children lying in the blossoming grasses read

Arthur Rimbaud

Their book of red morocco. Look, alas! but he,
Like myriad white angels, split up en route, has started
To saunter off away behind the mountain. She,
All cold and dark, runs on. After the male has parted.

IV

Regrets for young arms, thick with pure grass; for May
Moons, golden, within the holy bed's deep heart;
For joys of abandoned river lumberyards, the prey
To August evenings where the germs of slow rot start.

For the while, let her weep beneath the ramparts; sighs
Of poplars overhead are the only breezes now.
Sourceless, reflectionless and gray, this surface lies
Where some old dredger toils in his unmoving scow.

V

A toy in this sorry water's eye, I cannot reach—
My arms too short, my boat that its own mooring hinders—
One flower or the other; the yellow that beseeches
There, nor the blue, friends, in this water gray as cinders.

What powder of the willow trees, shaken by one wing!
The roses of these reeds, devoured now, a long time.
My boat still standing with its drawn chain tightening
In this watery rimless eye—in what deep slime?

Christian Morgenstern

THE KNEE

There wanders through the world a knee.
It's just a knee, no more.
It's not a tent; it's not a tree;
Only a knee, no more.

There was a man once in a war
Overkilled, killed fatally.
Alone, unhurt, remained the knee
Like a saint's relics, pure.

Since then it roams the whole world, lonely.
It is a knee, now, only.
It's not a tent; it's not a tree;
Only a knee, no more.

—translated with Lore Segal

THE MOUSETRAP

I

Palmstrom hasn't a crumb in the house;
Nevertheless, he has a mouse.

Von Korf, upset by his distress,
Builds a room of trellises

And places Palmstrom therewithin,
Fiddling an exquisite violin.

It gets late; the stars shine bright;
Palmstrom makes music in the night

Christian Morgenstern

Till, midway through the serenade,
In strolls the mouse to promenade.

Behind it, by some secret trick
A trapdoor closes, quiet, quick.

Palmstrom, before it, silently
Falls asleep, immediately.

II

Von Korf arrives in the early dawn
And loads this Useful Invention on

The nearest medium-sized, as it were,
Moving van for furniture,

Which is then hauled by a powerful horse,
Nimbly, into the distant forest.

There, profoundly isolated,
This strange couple are liberated:

First the mouse comes strolling out,
Then Palmstrom—after the mouse.

The animal, with no trace of fright,
Takes to its new home with delight.

Palmstrom, meanwhile, observing this,
Drives home with Korf, transformed by bliss.

—translated with Lore Segal

THE SPHERES

Palmstrom takes some paper from a drawer,
Distributing it artfully around the floor,

And after he has formed it into tight
Spheres, artfully distributed for the night,

He so distributes (for the night) these spheres
That he, when he wakes up suddenly in the night,

That he, waking in the dead of night, then hears
Paper crackling and a secret shuddering fright

Attacks him (so that in the night terrible fears
Attack him) being spooked by packing-paper spheres.

—translated with Lore Segal

PALMSTROM TO A NIGHTINGALE WHICH WOULD NOT LET HIM SLEEP

Why do you not transform
Yourself to a fish; and,
In this matter of song, perform
Accordingly? For otherwise,
Through the long nights, how can
Slumber restore my eyes
And blossom on my pillow,
Which is most needful? Then,
Do; if you are a noble fellow.

And your wife, too, on the nest—
How sweetly you will astound her
When you shine forth like a flounder

Blissfully at rest
On the top branch of your tree—
Or when you flutter around her
Like a flying mackerel.
Heavenly Philomel,
You will do me this courtesy?

—translated with Lore Segal

THE QUESTIONNAIRE

Korf gets a printed questionnaire
From the police, sternly worded,
Demanding who he is and how and where?

Where was his last home? Precisely what
Day of what year was he born?
Divorced, married or single? If not, why not?

Has he received a permit to live,
At all, here? If so, why? Where does
His money come from? What does he believe?

Should the opposite appear,
He will be placed under arrest.
Beneath, two names are signed: Borowsky and Rear.

Short and sweetly, Korf replies:
"My dear most high commissioner,
The undesigning herein certifies

That after a personal inspection
He has the honor to present himself
Non-existent under the Legislation,

Prior, exterior, and underhanded, with co-regret of
Proximitywise referentially discerned,
Korf. (To the police of the state of . . .)"

This stuns the Bureau Chief concerned.

—translated with Lore Segal

THE PIKE

Reformed by sainted Anthony,
A pike decided, morally,
Together with his wife and son,
To try and feed himself upon
The vegetarian ideal.

Since that day, he would only eat
Seagrass, searose and seaoatmeal.
Horrors! Soon as he had dined,
Seagrass, searose, creamofseawheat
Flowed out again horribly behind.

The pond was soon polluted, wholly;
Five hundred fish expired in pain.
Saint Anthony, however, when
Hurriedly summoned back again,
Said only, "Holy, holy, holy."

—translated with Lore Segal

Christian Morgenstern

THE WALLPAPER FLOWER

I am a wallpaper flower, fine,
Renewed, returning endlessly
—But not in May and bright moonshine—
On all four walls. You'll never see

Enough of me. You will pursue
Me 'round your little room, unspacious,
Bounding as Knights of the Chessboard do
Till you go nuts, my precious!

—translated with Lore Segal

Rainer Maria Rilke

from SONNETS TO ORPHEUS

I, 1

A tree rose up. O clear transcendency!
O Orpheus sings! A tall tree in the ear.
All things were hushed. Yet even silently
New origins, beckonings and change appear.
Creatures of silence crowded from the clear
Released wood out of burrow, den and lair.
It turned out they were not so hushed within
Themselves from cunning nor so stilled with fear

But with their listening. Bellow, shriek and roar
Seemed little in their hearts. And where had been
Scarcely a hut to take that in before,
A shelter, hidden from their dark desiring,
Having an entryway whose timbers tremble—
You founded temples for them in their hearing.

I, 2

And nearly a girl it was, then, issuing
From this harmonious joy of song and lyre,
And shining clearly through her veils of Spring
She made herself a bed inside my ear.
And slept in me. And all things were her sleep.
The trees, that always had astonished me,
Tangible distances, the meadow felt,
Every wondering that had surprised my self.

She slept the world. How ever did you so
Achieve her, singing god, that she'd not long
To waken first? See, she arose and slept.
Where is her death? O find out this theme yet
Before your singing is consumed in song!
Where does she sink from me . . . a girl almost . . .

I, 3

A god is able. But a mere man, through
The tight lyre, tell me, how can a man follow?
Your mind is cleavage. And wherever two
Heart roads cross, no temple stands to Apollo.
To sing by his schooling is not desire;
No courting something gotten in the end.
Singing is Being. And simple to his lyre.
But we, when are we? When does the god spend

Earth and all stars in our Being? Poet,
Youngster, it's not this, not your first love's care,
Although your mouth flew open. Learn to forget,
Forget the sudden singing. It will dwindle.
The real song is a different breath. An air
For nothing. Drifting in the god. A wind.

I, 4

O you who are tender, step now and then
Into the breath that does not notice you;
Touching your cheeks, let it be drawn in two
To tremble behind you and be one again.
You who are sound, O you who have the luck,
You who seem to be beginning hearts.
Bows for the darts and targets of the darts,
More endlessly shine the smiles that your tears have marked.

Never fear suffering. The heaviness—
You may return it to the earth's own weight;
The mountains are heavy, heavy the seas.
You could not sustain even the trees
Your childhood planted, long since grown too great.
Ah, but the breezes . . . O the spaciousness . . .

I, 5

Erect no gravestone to his memory;
Just let the rose bloom for his sake each year.
For it is Orpheus. His metamorphosis
In this one and this one. We needn't worry
For other names. Now and for all time
It's Orpheus when there's song. He comes and goes.
Isn't it much already if sometimes
He overstays, a few days, the bowl of roses?

For you to grasp it, he must disappear!
Though he, himself, takes fright at vanishing.
Even while his word exceeds existence here
He's gone already ways you cannot trace.
The lyre's lattice does not bind his hands.
Even in overstepping, he obeys.

I, 6

Does he come from here? No, from both realms
Has his broad nature grown.
More masterfully would he bend the willows' limbs
Who willows' roots had known.
On the table, leave, when you go to bed,
No bread or milk; it will draw the dead.
But him, the necromancer, let him blend,
Under the mildness of the eyelid,

Their aspect in the look of everything.
Let earthsmoke and mystery, in their magic,
Be true to him as the most mordant logic.
For him there must be nothing that can damage,
Whether from rooms or graves, the valid image;
Let him praise jug, clasp and finger-ring.

I, 7

Praising, that's it! Chosen to praise,
He came like ore out of the stone's
Silence. His heart, the ephemeral press,
For men, of an eternal wine.
In the godlike example's grip
His voice does not fall into drought.
All turns vineyard, all turns grape,
Ripened in his sensitive South.

No mold in the Imperial Vaults
Gives the lie to his praising, nor
That from the gods a shadow falls.
He is one messenger who stays;
Who still holds, into the door
Of the dead, bowls with fruits worth praise.

I, 8

Only in areas of Praise may walk
Mourning, nymph of the fountain wept,
To see that our downfall is kept
Clear even to the selfsame rock
That bears the gateways and the altars.
Look, the feeling she's the youngest one
Among the siblings of the spirit dawns
Just now around her quiet shoulders.

Rejoicing knows, Longing is compliant—
Mourning alone still learns; like maidenhands
She counts up all night long the ancient curse.
Yet suddenly, aslant, unpracticed even,
She lifts a constellation of our voice,
Unclouded by her breath, into the Heavens.

I, 9

He only who has raised
Among the shadows, too, his lyre,
Foretells and can restore
Unceasing praise.
Who with the dead has eaten
Their poppy, he alone
Will never lose again
The lightest tone.

Though the reflection in the pool
Often before our eyes is swimming,
Know the image.
Nowhere but in the dual
Kingdom shall a voice become
Everlasting, calm.

I, 10

Antique sarcophagi, who have stayed
Always in my emotions, I greet you,
Whom jubilant waters of the Roman days,
Like a wandering song, flow through.
Or those, the opened ones, like eyes
Of some awakening, glad shepherd
—Full of silence and the bee-sucked herbs—
Where fluttered the enchanted butterflies.

Rainer Maria Rilke

All that a man extracts from doubt
I greet, the once-more opening mouths
That knew already what the silence meant.
Do we know, friends, or do we not?
The lingering hour molds them both
Into the face of man.

II, 4

The Tapestry of the Lady with the Unicorn

O this is the beast that does not have being!
But they did not know that. And then besides,
—The neck, the strong stance, the decisive strides,
And even to the still light of its seeing
—They loved it. And because they loved it (indeed,
It never was), a pure creature happened.
They allowed room, left always clear and opened,
Where it easily raised its head and had scarce need

To be. They fed it on no oats nor corn
But only on the chance it might be. Might.
Fodder that gave such force to the creature
It drove a horn out of its brow. One horn.
Then to a virgin came here, trotting white—
Was in the silver-mirror and in her.

AN ARCHAIC TORSO OF APOLLO

We will not ever know his legendary head
Wherein the eyes, like apples, ripened. Yet
His torso glows like a candelabra
In which his vision, merely turned down low,

Still holds and gleams. If this were not so, the curve
Of the breast could not so blind you, nor this smile
Pass lightly through the soft turn of the loins
Into that center where procreation flared.

If this were not so, this stone would stand defaced, maimed,
Under the transparent cascade of the shoulder,
Not glimmering that way, like a wild beast's pelt,

Nor breaking out of all its contours
Like a star; for there is no place here
That does not see you. You must change your life.

SLUMBERSONG

When I lose you, someday,
how will you sleep without me
whispering myself away
above you like the linden tree?

Without me waking to lay down
words, as close as eyelids,
upon your breasts, upon
your limbs, upon your lips?

Without my closing you to leave
you alone with what is yours,
like a garden with its sheaves
of melissas and of anise-stars?

Rainer Maria Rilke

THE PANTHER

In the Botanical Gardens, Paris

Always passing bars has dulled
His sight so, it will hold no more.
For him, there are a thousand bars;
Behind the thousand bars, no world.

The soft walk of his strong, lithe strides
Turns in the smallest of all orbits
Like the dance of force around an axis
Where a great will stands stupefied.

Only sometimes, the curtain of his eye
Lifts, soundlessly—an image enters,
That runs through his tense, arrested members
Into the heart, to die.

Corrado Govoni

THE VILLAGES

A sympathy of bells explodes
From a white bell-tower above
The gray roofs. Out of a large oven
Women with red kerchiefs pull the loaves.

In the new snow they've brought a pig
To slaughter; around, enchanted by
The blood, children wait for that quick
Cruel agony, with big eyes.

The cocks all peal trimphantly.
Oxen come from the black hay-barns,
Spreading over the banksides, quietly,

Then go down, grave, to drink the silver water.
In the fields, pink and white, the graveyards
Shine among the green waves of the wheat.

Federico García Lorca

SOMNAMBULIST BALLAD

Green, how I need you now, green.
Green breezes and the branches green.
The small boat far out at sea.
The pony in the high sierra.
With shadows on her waistband
She dreams on her veranda,
Green her skin and the hair green
With eyes of icy silver.
Green, how I need you now, green.
Under the gypsy moon,
Things are staring at her,
Things that she can't see.

Green, how I need you now, green.
Gigantic stars of hoarfrost
Come with the fish of shadows
Opening the high road of dawn.
The fig tree scrapes the breeze
With sandpaper of its branches.
A filching cat, the mountain,
Bristles its acrid spikes.
Who's coming, though? And from where?
She's dreaming on her veranda,
Green her skin and the hair green,
She dreams of the bitter sea.

"Old friend, I want to barter
This horse of mine for your house,
My saddle for your mirror,
My dagger for your quilt.
Old friend, I have come bleeding
From the passes of Cabra."
"If I might, still, my boy,
We would strike up this bargain.

But I am no longer I
Nor my house, now, my own house."
"Good friend, I want to die
Decently in my own bed—
If it might be, made of steel,
With the linens of fine holland.
Can't you see the wound I've taken
From my breastbone to my throat?"
"You wear on your white shirt
Three hundred swarthy roses.
Your blood comes oozing, pungent,
On all sides of your sash.
But I am no longer I
Nor my house, now, my own house."
"Let me at least, then, climb
Up to the high verandas;
Let me climb, then, only climb
Up to the green verandas,
Handrailings of the moonlight
Where the voice of water sounds."

Now the two friends are climbing
Up to the high verandas
Leaving a trail of blood,
Leaving a trail of tears.
Tiny lanterns of tin
Were trembling on the rooftops.
A thousand tambourines
Of crystal lacerate the daybreak.

Green, how I need you now, green.
Green breezes and the branches green.
The two friends have gone up.
A long-drawn wind was leaving
A strange taste on the tongue
Of gall, of mint and sweet basil.
"Old friend, where is she, tell me

Federico García Lorca

Where is your bitter daughter?"
"She waited so often for you—
How often she would be waiting,
Her face fresh and her hair black,
Here on this green veranda."

There on the face of the cistern
The gypsy girl was rocking.
Green her skin and the hair green,
With eyes of icy silver.
An icicle of the moon
Sustains her on the water.
The night turned intimate
As a little village square.
Drunken civil guards
Were pounding down the door.
Green, how I need you now, green.
Green breezes and the branches green.
The small boat far out at sea.
The pony in the high sierra.

Yehuda Amichai

DOG AFTER LOVE

After you walked out,
I let a bloodhound sniff at my chest,
Sniff at my belly. His nostrils filled,
He'll start off on your trail.

May he track down and lacerate
Your best beloved's scrotum, snap off
His virile portions or, at least then, fetch me
One sock between his teeth that once was yours.

Leszek Szaruga

LICENTIA POETICA

1.

The gravest threat
lurks in the library. It is essential
older newspapers be burned; essential
yesterday's newspapers be burned. Yesterday's
weathercast has been proven
true. Has been proven
false. By today, one no longer
knows what it was actually like.
One does know for certain
it was not what should have been.
A deviation.

      Only
the present permits
true reconstruction of the past. Only
today can we predict
what happened yesterday. Memory
is an undemonstrable presumption.

2.

The gravest threat
lurks in poetry. It is essential
to ban all words; essential
to ban even pauses. Pauses
mean something. Silence
means something. Therefore it is essential
we prohibit silence.

—translated with Kathleen Snodgrass, Peter
Lengyel, and Justyna Kostkowska

Leszek Szaruga

BETWEEN

for Stanislaw Baranczak

Between the right to a voice and the voice
of right
poems break out of their shell,
hope's ravens, all pure white.

Between the power of righteousness and the right
to power
suffering's stanzas hatch out
truth's bitter shrubs come to light.

Between the voice of power and the power
of the voice
the whisper rises of the powerless
stifled by powers with no right.

—translated with Justyna Kostkowska

PENAL COLONY

Once upon a time,
the Correctional Colony F. Kafka
came to be Arkady. We
will dream of it our dreams
singing with a steady beat:

LABOR CREATES LIBERTY
FREEDOM EQUALS
RECOGNIZED NECESSITY

Leszek Szaruga

Dreaming, singing that song since
the Correctional Colony F. Kafka
is battening inside us.

Battening with a steady beat.

—translated with Justyna Kostkowka

Marin Sorescu

I BOUND UP THE TREES' EYES

I bound up the trees' eyes
With a green babushka
And told the trees to find me.

And, right off, the trees found me
In an outburst of leaves.

I bound up the small birds' eyes
With a scarf of clouds
And told the birds to find me.

And the small birds found me
In a song.

I bound up the eyes of sorrow
With a smile
And the next day sorrow found me
In a certain love.

I bound up the sun's eyes
With my own nights
And told the sun to find me.

You're over there, the sun said,
Right back of that time span.
Don't hide out any more.

Don't hide out any more,
All of those things told me;
So did all those feelings
Whose eyes
I'd kept trying to bind.

—translated with Dona Roşu and Luciana Costea

Marin Sorescu

PEASANTS

At home they boil, then eat, grain that's been stored,
Making a little fire of ash and straw.
Hamsters themselves—forgive them for it, Lord—
They haul back less and less grain in their craw.

Yet all their pockets, like thieves', have been checked
When they come, starving, from the fields of grain.
These peasants waste a lot that they collect
By a bad habit—eating—they still retain.

A further problem is created by
This class for the finances of our state:
Our peasants simply will not multiply;
The species falls off at an alarming rate.

Right now when all this land is theirs—why,
What's wrong with them? They mope, they weep, they die.

—translated with Dona Roşu and Luciana Costea

SHAKESPEARE

Shakespeare created the world in seven days.
First day, he made the heavens, the mountains and the
            spiritual abyss.
Second day, he made the rivers, seas, the oceans
And the other passions—
Giving them to Hamlet, Julius Caesar, to Antony,
            Cleopatra and Ophelia,
To Othello and to others,
So they could master them, they and their descendants
To all eternity.
Third day, he gathered all peoples

And taught them flavors:
The flavor of happiness, of love, of desperation,
The flavor of jealousy, of glory and so forth,
Till all the flavors had been gone through.
Then certain characters turned up late.
The creator, in compassion, patted them on the head
And told them there was nothing left but to make themselves
Literary critics
And refute his works.
The fourth and fifth days were reserved for laughter.
He launched the clowns
To cut some somersaults
And permitted kings, emperors
And other miserables to entertain themselves.
The sixth day he solved certain administrative problems:
He staged a tempest
And taught King Lear
How to wear a crown of straw.
Some leftovers remained from the world's creation
So he created Richard Third.
The seventh day he looked around to see what's left to do.
Already theater managers had filled up the world with posters
And Shakespeare thought that after so much hard work
He surely deserved to see a show himself.
But first, since he was much too tired,
He went to die a little.

—translated with Dona Roşu and Luciana Costea

THIEVES

I used to have a poem that wouldn't let me sleep
So I sent it to a Grandpa
In the country.

Marin Sorescu

After that, I wrote another
And sent it to my Mom
To keep it in the attic.

Later, I kept on writing others
And, with sinking heart, bestowed them with relatives
Who promised the best care for them.

So then, each new poem
Had someone to take it in
Since each of my friends
Has, in turn, another friend
You can trust to keep a secret.

So I don't know by now
Where this or that verse is.
And should the thieves come to my house,
However much they'd torture me,
I could say nothing but
They are in a safe place
Somewhere in this country.

—translated with Dona Roşu and Luciana Costea

FORTRESS

I am a citadel, almost stately,
That I have to reconquer
Down to its last stone
Every morning.

Filled with hatred,
I work up close to it
Then, practicing this and that deception,

Start clambering up its walls,
Shredding my knees
And spitting out my innards.

Once up there, I'm exhausted
But until late in the evening,
Inexhaustibly stubborn,
I rain down on myself, the day-old self,
Stone blocks
And boiling pine tar.

—translated with Dona Roşu and Luciana Costea

AN AMŒBA

"What's new?"
The Moon one day
Asked Earth.

For millions of years
She'd watched him working away,
Moving seas from one continent
To another,
Experimenting with glaciers and volcanoes
And daily ruining a multitude of mountains.
"What's new?"
She repeated.

Worn out, he answered gravely,
"An amœba."

The Moon knitted up her brows then,
Pretending to understand
The mystery of life and creation,

And went off thinking,
"Men—their little foibles!"

> —translated with Dona Roşu and Luciana Costea

BEHIND CLOSED DOORS

This woman
Has someone in her bathroom.

She talks to me,
She loves me truly,
But someone, behind closed doors,
keeps monkeying with her soul.
I can read in her eyes,
Her hair,
The life line of her palm
That this house has just one entrance,
That she's hiding someone in her bathroom.
Or, anyway, next door,
Somewhere in this street,
In another city or a forest,
Or on the ocean floor.

Somebody's hiding there,
Spying on my thoughts,
Hearing my timeless sentiments,
Checking their watch.

> —translated with Dona Roşu and Luciana Costea

Ion Mircea

SIBIU IN MIST

Too much in the light, the first part of my life,
My body's a film, more and more faded, unrecognizable,
And mist nibbles away its edges.
In the Goldsmith's Market there's a mist.
I climb the Fingerling Stairs, in mist,
A dance, Wallachian, with ankle bells,
From the sixteenth century, in mist.

I go on, passing a clocksmith's shop;
Again, dark comes on early
And there's mist.
A light inside turns its window to the crystal
Of a monstrous clock, all threads and wisps;
Behind, a face peers out at passersby
Through the clock's hands, in the mist.

Since it's all over now, for good,
And, eddying more softly toward me, night arrives,
I gather in these byways toward the center—
And from that focal point (as from some new way to exist)
The same old landscape with its mist,
As through an ancient magnifying glass, revives.

—translated with Dona Roşu and Luciana Costea

II.
FOLK SONGS AND BALLADS

French Folk Ballad

THE WHITE DOE

They go, go to the wood;
The mother and the daughter.

The old mother would sing;
The fair daughter is sighing.

"Then speak: why do you sigh,
My daughter Marguerita?"

"The long raging within,
I dare tell of it never.

"A fair maiden by day,
A white doe am I nightly.

"The chase rides on my track,
The barons and the princes.

"My own brother, Renaud,
He rides there to my sorrow.

"Then go, mother, then go—
Turn back quickly to tell him

"To call, call back his hounds
Till full noonday tomorrow."

"Renaud, where are your hounds;
Renaud, where are the huntsmen?"

"They go, go to the wood;
The white doe they go coursing."

French Folk Ballad

"Renaud, call back your hounds;
Renaud, call back the huntsmen."

He sounds, sounds his bright horn,
Full three calls of his trumpet.

The third call of his horn,
The white doe has been taken.

"To pare deerskin so fine,
Now call, call our game skinner."

The old deerskinner speaks:
"I know not what to tell you—

"Her hair shows to be blond;
Her breast, some fair maid's bosom."

The man draws out his blade;
The white doe's cut and quartered.

He carves, slicing the feast
For barons and for princes.

"We've all gathered save one—
My sister Marguerita."

"Then turn, fall to your feast;
I'm here seated before you.

"My head lies on the plate;
My heart lies with the leavings;

"My heart's blood has been poured,
Spilled out over the kitchen;

French Folk Ballad

"On black coals at your grate,
My poor bones still are burning."

—translated with Paul Archambault

Five Hungarian Folk Songs

THE BAD WIFE

Hurry home now, dearest mother;
He's so sick—our poor old father.
   Wait, daughter, wait a bit;
   I'll just dance a little bit;
   I'll come home directly.
   Just another turn or so
   Then you can expect me.

Hurry home now, dearest mother;
We just called the holy father.
   Wait, daughter, wait a bit;
   I'll just dance a little bit;
   I'll come home directly.
   Just another turn or so
   Then you can expect me.

Hurry home now, dearest mother;
He just died—our dear old father.
   Wait daughter, wait a bit;
   I'll just dance a little bit;
   I'll come home directly.
   Just another turn or so
   Then you can expect me.

Hurry home now, dearest mother;
We just buried our dear father.
   Ay! Ay! My one sheet!
   My beautiful white sheet!
   Other men I'm sure to meet
   But I can't get such a sheet—
   Since I never learned to sew
   I just can't make such a sheet!

TIME TO SETTLE DOWN NOW

Time to settle down now; it's just necessary;
All I need to know is who I ought to marry.
Jai-jai-jai, Jai-ja-jai, who I ought to marry.

If I take a young wife, she won't know her stitches;
I'd feel too ashamed, then, wearing boughten breeches.
Jai-jai-jai, Jai-ja-jai, wearing boughten breeches.

If I take an old wife, she'd be glum and gloomy;
Every word would rumble, black as thunder to me.
Jai-jai-jai, Jai-ja-jai, black as thunder to me.

If I take a poor wife, we'll have debts and trouble;
What's the use in making one poor beggar double?
Jai-jai-jai, Jai-ja-jai, one poor beggar double!

If I take a rich wife, nagging—that's our future:
"You're just sponging off me, good-for-nothing moocher!"
Jai-jai-jai, Jai-ja-jai, good-for-nothing moocher!

Dear good Lord, dear good Lord, help to set me straight, now;
Should I still stay single; should I take a mate, now?
Jai-jai-jai, Jai-ja-jai, should I take a mate, now?

I've got only one hope really life-sustaining:
Single life still suits me; that's why I'm remaining.
Jai-jai-jai, Jai-ja-jai, that's why I'm remaining.

CARRIAGE, WAGON, CARRIAGE, SLED

Carriage, wagon, carriage, sled;
This year I've still, *libilibi lim lom, lomzati bom bom,*
Not got wed.

Next year if I'm living still,
I'll get hitched if, *libilibi lim lom, lomzati bom bom,*
Some man will.

If none takes me, I won't roam;
I'll just go on, *libilibi lim lom, lomzati bom bom,*
Right at home.

IF I CLIMBED THAT MOUNTAIN

If I climbed that mountain I'd discover, oh,
I could find me more than just one lover, so
It's bad, bad, bad, too darn bad
My girl's got a heart that runs like butter, oh!

Trouble is, I wouldn't want another, though;
I'd be lost without my last year's lover, so
It's bad, bad, bad, too darn bad
My girl's got a heart that runs like butter, oh!

NEAR THE CSITAR MOUNTAIN FOOTHILLS

Near the Csitar Mountain foothills, far away and long ago,
Someone said your horse once stumbled in the year's first fall
of snow.
      In your hand you broke a bone;
      You can't hold me for your own.
So it's clear, my dearest lover, I could not be yours alone.

Through the skies a bird goes flying—to and fro I see him dart.
How I long to send a letter far away to my sweetheart!
      Little birdie, if you may,
      Take this letter on your way;
Go and tell my dearest lover not to weep for me that way.

There's an ash grove standing yonder—ay, it stands so very far!
At the center, at the center, two rosemary bushes are.
      By my shoulder one bends near;
      One is bending toward my dear;
So you see, my dearest lover, I'll be yours someday, that's clear.

Two Romanian Folk Ballads

THE EWE LAMB

Near a low foothill
At Heaven's doorsill,
Where the trail's descending
To the plain and ending,
Here three shepherds keep
Their three flocks of sheep,
One, Moldavian,
One, Hungarian,
And one, Vrancean.
Now, the Vrancean
And Hungarian
In their thoughts, conniving,
Have laid plans, contriving
At the close of day
To ambush and slay
The Moldavian;
He, the wealthier man,
Had more flocks to keep,
Handsome, long-horned sheep,
Horses, trained and sound,
Fierce and loyal hounds.
One small ewe lamb, though,
Dappled gray as tow,
While three full days passed
Bleated loud and fast,
Would not touch the grass.
"Ewe lamb, dapple-gray,
Muzzled black and gray,
While three full days passed
You bleat loud and fast;
Don't you like this grass?
Are you too sick to eat,
Little lamb so sweet?"
"Oh, my master dear,

Drive the flock out near
That field, dark to view,
Where the grass grows new,
Where there's shade for you.
Master, master dear,
Call a large hound near,
A fierce one and fearless,
Strong, loyal and peerless.
The Hungarian
And the Vrancean
When the daylight's through
Mean to murder you."
"Lamb, my little ewe,
If this omen's true,
If I'm doomed to death
On this tract of heath,
Tell the Vrancean
And Hungarian
To let my bones lie
Somewhere here close by,
By the sheepfold here
So my flocks are near,
Back of my hut's grounds
So I'll hear my hounds.
Tell them what I say:
There, beside me lay
One small pipe of beech
With its soft, sweet speech,
One small pipe of bone
With its loving tone,
One of elderwood,
Fiery-tongued and good.
Then when the winds blow
They'll play on them so
All my listening sheep
Would draw near and weep

Tears, no blood so deep.
How I met my death,
Tell them not a breath;
Say I could not tarry,
Say I've gone to marry
A princess—my bride
Is the whole world's pride.
Say a star fell, bright,
For my wedding night;
Sun and moon came down
To hold my bridal crown,
Firs and maple trees
Were my guests; my priests
Were the mountains high;
Fiddlers, birds that fly,
All birds of the sky;
Torchlights, stars on high.
But if you see there,
Should you meet somewhere,
My old mother, little,
With her white wool girdle,
Eyes with their tears flowing,
Over the plains going,
Asking one and all,
Saying to them all,
'Who has ever known,
Who has seen my own
Shepherd fine to see,
Slim as a willow tree,
With his dear face, bright
As the milk-foam white,
His small mustache, right
As the young wheat's ear,
With his hair so dear,
Like plumes of the crow,
Little eyes that glow

Like the ripe, black sloe?'
Ewe lamb, small and pretty,
For her sake have pity;
Let it just be said
I have gone to wed
A princess most noble
There on Heaven's doorsill.
To that mother, old,
Let it not be told
That a star fell, bright,
For my bridal night;
Firs and maple trees
Were my guests; my priests
Were the mountains high;
Fiddlers, birds that fly,
All birds of the sky;
Torchlights, stars on high."

—translated with Ioan and Kitty Popa,
Radu Lupan and Simona Draghici

MASTER BUILDER MANOLE

I.

Downstream on the wide
Argesh River's side
Negru Voda's riding;
Ten men go beside him:
Masons, craftsmen fine,
Master builders—nine;
Manole makes ten,
The greatest craftsman.
Down this dale, they're bound
To erect and found
A monastery hall,
A memorial.
There, as they passed on,
Soon they came upon
A poor shepherd lad
Piping *doinas*, sad.
Stopping to behold him,
Negru Voda told him:
"Worthy shepherd lad,
Piping *doinas*, sad,
Up the Argesh where
You drove your flocks there,
Down the Argesh, too,
Where flocks went with you—
Have you, wandering there,
Noticed anywhere
An unfinished wall
Ruined, shunned by all,
Near a hazel copse
On a green hill's slopes?"
"Yes, my lord, it's true;
I saw, passing through,

An unfinished wall
Ruined, shunned by all.
Soon as my dogs see it,
They draw back and flee it,
Bark at it with dread,
Howl as at the dead."
When he'd heard the lad,
The voivode felt glad
And, turning straightway,
Set his steps that way
With the masons, fine,
Master builders—nine;
And Manole, ten,
The greatest craftsman.
"Here's my wall, you see!
This site I decree
My monastery hall,
My memorial.
You stonemasons, then,
Masters, journeymen,
Set at once to work;
Let no man here shirk;
One and all must build
The great shrine I've willed—
My monastery hall,
My memorial.
I'll make you rich, then—
Boyars, landed men.
But if not, I swear
I'll seal you up there
In the cloister's wall
Living, one and all!"

II.

The men, hurrying,
Stretched their measuring string,
Marked out all the grounds,
Dug deep trenches down,
Working without pause
So the great wall rose.
Yet all they set upright
Crumbled that same night.
Second day the same,
Then third day the same,
The fourth day again,
They worked on in vain.
Negru Voda wondered,
Scowling black as thunder;
He would rage and scold them,
Then once more he told them
He would seal them all,
Living, in the wall!
The great builders, then,
Masons and craftsmen
Shivering, worrying,
Went on working, hurrying
The whole summer's day
Till the dusk fell, gray;
Manole drew aside,
Let his labors bide,
Laid down near the stream
Where he dreamt a dream.
When at last he woke
This is what he spoke:
"Masons, craftsmen fine,
Master builders nine,
Would you hear the dream
I've dreamt by this stream?

A breath from on high
Warned me—I won't lie—
Build the best we might,
It would fall each night
Till we swear, one and all,
To seal in this wall
Any sister dear,
Any wife most dear,
Who may first appear
The next morning here
Bringing bread and meat
For her man to eat.
So if you believe
We must now achieve
This monastery hall,
This memorial,
We must then prepare,
One and all, to swear
Each will keep his oath,
Keep this secret close,
And the sister dear,
Or that wife most dear,
Who appears next morning
Must be, without warning,
Sacrificed by us all,
Sealed up in the wall."

III.

See, when the day breaks
Then Manole wakes
And climbs up the stakes
Of the wattled fence;
From the scaffold thence,
Scans the field below

And the road also.
Now, what might appear?
What was coming near?
His own wife so dear,
The flower of the field,
Bringing him his meal,
Wine to drink and meat
For her man to eat.
She was drawing near.
Seeing her so clear,
His heart beat with fear;
He knelt down with dread
Then, weeping, he said:
"Grant, Lord, to the world
Fierce rain, foaming, swirled
Into small streams gushing
Till great torrents, rushing,
Swell the waters so
My love stops below.
Down the valley, force
My love off her course."
In mercy, the Lord
Heard Manole's word,
Gathered clouds on high,
Darkening the sky.
Suddenly, down hurled
Fierce rain, foaming, swirled
Into small streams gushing
Till great torrents, rushing,
Made the waters swell.
Yet, though torrents fell,
No rainfall could force
His love off her course;
Closer still she crept.
Where Manole kept
Watch, his poor heart wept

And he bowed down then
To pray once again:
"Dear Lord, let winds blow
On this earth below;
Uproot the great firs,
Bend the sycamores,
Turn the mountains over
But turn back my lover.
Down the valley, force
My love off her course."
In mercy, the Lord
Heard Manole's word,
Made a great wind blow
On the earth below
Bending sycamores,
Uprooting great firs,
Turning mountains over,
But Anna, his lover,
Held fast to her track,
Still would not turn back.
Down the road she wavered
Yet drew nearer ever,
Till—grief and despair!—
See, at last she's there.

IV.

The great builders, nine,
Masons, craftsmen fine,
Seeing her there, they were
Glad that it was her.
Manea, half insane,
Kissed her all the same,
In his arms embraced her,
Up the scaffold raised her,

On the wall he placed her
And joking, addressed her:
"Hold still, little love;
What are you scared of?
Just in fun, we'll all
Build you in the wall."
Trusting in him, she
Just laughed merrily.
Manea sighed hard,
But soon had to start
At his work and build
Till the dream's fulfilled.
Now the wall was raised
Till she stood embraced
To her ankles, trim,
To her calves, so slim,
While she, the poor thing,
Her smile vanishing,
Kept on murmuring:
"Manole, Manole,
Good Master Manole!
It's gone far enough;
This joke's no good, love.
Manole, Manole,
Good Master Manole!
The wall's hurting me,
Crushing my body!"
Manea just stood, stilled,
Then went on to build;
Now the wall was raised
Till she stood embraced
To her ankles, trim,
To her calves, so slim,
To her ribs and chest,
To her little breasts.
She, though, the poor thing,

Weeping, sorrowing,
Kept on murmuring:
"Manole, Manole,
Good Master Manole!
The wall's hurting me;
My breasts cry hopelessly;
It's crushing my baby!"
Manole, half berserk,
Kept on at his work
So the wall was raised
Till she stood, embraced
To her ribs and chest,
To her little breasts,
Then up to her lips,
And to her eyelids,
So, poor thing, the men
Saw her no more then
Yet they always heard
From the wall, those words:
"Manole, Manole,
Good Master Manole!
The wall's crushing me;
Life's snuffed out of me!"

V.

Downstream on the wide
Argesh River's side,
Negru Voda rides
To pray, to kneel down
In this cloister's ground,
By this splendid, tall
Monastery hall,
Stateliest of all.
Viewing this fine sight,

Two Romanian Folk Ballads

The Prince felt delight
And he spoke this then:
"You masons, craftsmen,
Master builders ten,
Speak up truthfully,
Hand on heart, tell me
Whether you're so skilled
That you might yet build
One more cloister hall,
A memorial,
Of still greater height,
More splendid, more bright?"
The great builders, then,
Masons, journeymen,
Who were standing by
On the roof-beam, high,
One and all replied,
Joyous, full of pride:
"Such master craftsmen,
Masons, journeymen,
Builders of our worth
Can't be found on earth.
Know this: we are skilled
So that we can build
Anything that's willed—
One more cloister hall,
A memorial
Stateliest of all."
Negru Voda heard,
Thought about their words,
Then he gave commands:
"Pull the scaffold stands
And ladders down, then.
And as for the ten
Builders and craftsmen,
Let them stay, forgotten

Till they're dead and rotten
Where the roof-beam, high,
Juts against the sky."
The builders thought, afraid,
Then designed and made
Out of shingles, light,
Wings to give them flight.
They stretched these out, there,
Leaped out in thin air,
But they fell like rock
And where each man struck
There his body broke.
Meantime, poor Manole,
Good Master Manole,
When finally he tried
To hurl himself wide,
Heard a voice that sighed,
A voice from the wall,
A voice, muffled, small,
Well-loved and well-known,
Echoing a moan,
Murmuring on and on:
"Manole, Manole,
Good Master Manole!
The wall's crushing me;
My breasts cry hopelessly;
It's crushing my baby;
Life's snuffed out of me!"
When he heard her speak
Manole sank, weak;
All his sight spun, twirling,
The great clouds were swirling
And the world turned, whirling;
From there, where the high
Roof juts in the sky,
Dead, Manole fell;

Two Romanian Folk Ballads

But what else, as well,
In that place befell?
A small fountain keeping
Peaceful waters seeping,
Calm salt waters steeping,
A spring fed by weeping!

—translated with Ioan and Kitty Popa
and with Radu Lupan

Four Romanian Folk Songs

YOU FULL BOTTLE, HERE'S A KISS

You full bottle, here's a kiss;
Why stick me in the mud like this?
Bottle empty or filled up;
I go to bed, I get up.
I'd build my house lovingly;
This full bottle won't let me.
House and stable, carefully;
Bottle just won't pity me.
Make a good house and a stable;
Bottle says I'm just not able.

HOLY FATHER, WORTHY PRIEST

Holy father, worthy priest,
Answer me one question, please:
A little wife that still looks good,
May she make love when she could?
A wife that's married to a man,
May she make love when she can?
"Both with me, and you also,
Only not a soul must know;
Both with me and with another
But her man must not discover,
Nor the town, she's got a lover;
Both with me and anyone,
With the priest from the next town—
That's forgiven soon, at least,
Since it's no sin with the priest."

Two Romanian Folk Songs

OH MY SWEETHEART, MY POOR BABY

Oh my sweetheart, my poor baby,
She spins thread just like fence pickets,
Cloth like hedges made of wickets,
Like farm gates, rough-cut and thickest;
If next to my skin I stick it,
It pricks like a wicker thicket.
My sweetheart is good at labor
But she shares the cuckoo's nature
When it sings in the daybreak
Getting my sweetheart awake.
Once the sun's up, she'll be found
Still in bed, securely bound
By quilts and blankets all around.

POOR, UNHAPPY LONG-HORNED OX HEADS

Poor, unhappy, long-horned ox heads;
How they marry off us blockheads!
And with money—wretched stuff!—
Lazy girls get married off.
Craving money drove me crazy;
I, too, took a girl that's lazy.
If I tell her I want fed,
She brings soiled plates for my bread
And spoons from underneath the bed.

—translated with Ioan and Kitty Popa

Seven German Folk Songs

WITHIN MY FATHER'S GARDEN

Within my father's garden
    Two little saplings grow;
The one of them bears nutmegs,
    The other one bears cloves.

The nutmeg's fresh and lovely,
    The cloves are sharp and sweet;
Now comes the time of parting,
    Never again to meet.

The winter's snows are melting;
    Far off these streams will flow.
Out of my sight you vanish,
    Out of my thoughts you go.

WE'VE GOT TO GO OFF TO THE WARS

We've got to go off to the wars
    And who knows when, my brothers?
We march out through the gates of town—
    Farewell, both Father and Mother.

Dear God, why are the heavens glowing
    Rose-red as burning coals?
It is the blood of soldiers flowing.
    Lord have mercy on our souls.

NINE TAILORS HELD A COUNCIL

Nine tailors held a council once
Out in the council yard;
All nine of them had places,
   Full nine times nine took places
Around a playing card.
           Veeda, veeda, veet, you Billygoat;
           Meck, meck, meck, you Tailor.

When all the nine were gathered there
Each man pulled up his stool,
Then all nine started drinking,
   Full nine times nine were drinking;
They drank a thimbleful.
           Veeda, veeda, veet. . . .

But when they got to their hotel
They couldn't get inside;
All nine of them went creeping,
   Full nine times nine went creeping
Right through the keyhole, wide.
           Veeda, veeda, veet. . . .

They held a jolly banquet then
When they got in the house,
And all nine tailors feasted,
   Full nine times nine, they feasted
Upon one French-fried louse.
           Veeda, veeda, veet. . . .

And when they got through eating there
They danced till they turned pale;
All nine of them were dancing,
   Full nine times nine were dancing
Upon one buck-goat's tail.
           Veeda, veeda, veet. . . .

And when they got through dancing there
They laughed, ha-ha-ha-ha!
They all nine fell a-sleeping,
   Full nine times nine were sleeping
Upon a blade of straw.
            Veeda, veeda, veet. . . .

And while they all were sleeping there
A mouse came rustling past;
All nine of them went creeping,
   Full nine times nine went creeping
Back through that keyhole, fast.
            Veeda, veeda, veet. . . .

To be a proper tailor, then,
You must weigh seven pounds.
Who doesn't weigh full seven,
   A solid, lusty seven,
His health cannot be sound.
            Veeda, veeda, veet, you Billygoat;
            Meck, meck, meck, you Tailor.

WHAT DO WE GEESE WEAR FOR CLOTHES?

Oh, what do we geese wear for clothes?
   Gi, ga, gock!
We march out barefoot, day and night,
Dressed in featherwear of white,
   Gi, ga, gock!
We've only got one smock!

What do we geese eat for food?
   Gi, ga, gack!
Summertimes we pick the meadow;
Winters, farm wives keep us fed, oh,

Gi, ga, gack!
Out of the oatmeal sack!

How do geese spend Martin's Mass?
  Gi, ga, geck!
Our keeper leads us from our pen
To Martin's schmaltzy feast and then,
  Gi, ga, geck!
It seems they wring our neck!

THREE STREET SONGS

i.

Whiner, squawker, snottysnout,
  Don't you go for that?
I sit in your house and guzzle,
Kiss your wife right in her muzzle;
  Don't you go for that?

ii.

Twixt the mountain and the dale
  There lies the open highway;
Who takes no care to keep my love
  Should turn me loose on my way.

Move on, move on; yours won't be missed.
  You've got free will and leeway.
There's many a long day left this year,
  And good luck's down each byway.

iii.

It's down to grass a maiden would—
   Nudge me, dearest Peter—
And there the little red rose stood.
   Nudge me now, fulfill your vow;
   If you can't, I'll show you how.
   Nudge me, dearest Peter.

Three Swedish Folk Songs

IN MY EIGHTEENTH YEAR

Once, at the time I was in my eighteenth year,
There came a handsome fellow; I fell in love, I fear.
I thought he'd be my own true love forever.

But all I believed then so swiftly passed away.
Another girl was there then and in his arms she lay;
I'm evermore in tears when I remember.

I hoped and believed you would be a friend to me,
But now I'm left abandoned for everyone to see.
I find no hope of joy on earth, forever.

Go find you a friend who's more faithful if you may;
May happiness go with you until your dying day;
I can't help dwell on days long gone and over.

I thank you for being my comfort and my rest.
I thank you for the times I have sheltered on your breast.
In Heav'n once more we two will be together.

WE'RE READY TO WANDER

We're ready to wander the woodlands afar
With our sheepflocks, our calves and our cows.
We wander the meadows, through moor and through marsh
To find richer grasslands our creatures may browse
On our march that we wait for so long.

Some days, on our grazing, the day seems so long;
I blow on my horn then a song.
With calves and with cattle, contented we roam . . .
Then turn back once more just as gladly for home,
To our kettles, our skillets and pans.

OH, PETER, DON'T GO JUST YET

Oh, Peter, don't go just yet;
Oh, Peter, don't go just yet.
Up the grain floor, up the barn loft,
Up the haymow lie down a little bit.
Uta-lu-la-lu! Uta-lu-la-lu!
It's not past twelve-thirty yet.
Yes, you up and counted the wrong hand;
Yes, you up and counted the long hand
And it's not twelve thirty yet.

III.
ART SONGS

Guilhem IX of Poitiers (Troubadour)

A NEW SONG FOR NEW DAYS

Such sweetness swells through these new days,
The woods take leaf; each bird must raise
In pure bird-latin of his kind,
The melody of a new song.
It's only just a man should find
His peace with what he's sought so long.

From her, where grace and beauty spring,
No message comes, no signet ring.
My heart can't rest and can't exult;
I don't dare move or take a stand
Until I know will peace result
And if she'll yield to my demands.

As for our love, you must know how
Love goes—it's like the hawthorn bough
That on the living tree stands, shaking
All night beneath the freezing rain
Till next day when the warm sun, waking,
Spreads through green leaves and boughs again.

That morning comes to mind once more
We two made peace in our long war;
She, in good grace, was moved to give
Her ring to me with true love's oaths.
God grant me only that I live
To get my hands beneath her clothes!

I can't stand their vernacular
Who keep my love from me afar.
By way of words, I guess I've found
A little saying that runs rife:
Let others mouth their loves around;
We've got the bread, we've got the knife.

Guilhem IX of Poitiers

LADIES WITH CATS

While sound asleep, I'll walk along
In sunshine, making up my song.
Some ladies get the rules all wrong;
    I'll tell you who:
The ones that turn a knight's love down
    And scorn it, too.

Grave mortal sins such ladies make
Who won't love for a true knight's sake;
And they're far worse, the ones who'll take
    A monk or priest—
They ought to get burned at the stake
    At very least.

Down in Auvergne, past Limousin,
Out wandering on the sly, I ran
Into the wives of Sir Guarin
    And Sir Bernard;
They spoke a proper welcome then
    By St. Leonard.

One said in her own dialect,
"Sir Pilgrim, may the Lord protect
Men so sweet-mannered, so correct,
    With such fine ways;
This whole world's full of lunatics
    And rogues these days."

For my reply—I'll swear to you
I didn't tell them *Bah* or *Boo*,
I answered nothing false or true;
    I just said, then,
"Babario, babariew,
    Babarian."

Then Agnes said to Ermaline,
"Let's take him home quick; don't waste time.
He's just the thing we hoped to find:
    Mute as a stone;
No matter what we've got in mind,
    It won't get known."

Beneath her cloak, one let me hide;
We slipped up to her room's fireside.
By now, I thought one could abide
    To play this role;
Right willingly I warmed myself
    At their live coals.

They served fat capons for our fare—
I didn't stop at just one pair.
We had no cook or cook's boy there,
    But just us three.
The bread was white, the pepper hot,
    The wine flowed free.

"Wait, sister, this could be a fake;
He might play dumb just for our sake.
Go see our big red cat's awake
    And fetch him, quick.
Right here's one silence we should break
    If it's a trick."

So Agnes brought that wicked beast,
Mustachioed, huge and full of yeast;
To see him sitting at our feast
    Seemed far from good;
I very nearly lost my nerve
    And hardihood.

We'd had our fill of drink and food,
So I undressed, as they thought good.
They brought that vile cat where I stood—
    My back was turned—
And then they raked him down my side
    From stem to stern.

Next, all at once, they yanked his tail
To make him dig in, tooth and nail;
I got a hundred scars, wholesale,
    Right then and there.
They could have flayed me, though, before
    I'd budge one hair.

So Agnes said to Ermaline,
"Sister, he's mute for sure; that's fine.
Let's take a nice warm bath, unwind,
    Then take things slow."
I stayed inside their oven there
    Eight days or so.

I screwed them, fairly to relate,
A full one hundred eighty-eight.
My breech-strap near broke at that rate,
    Also my reins.
I can't recount all my distress
    Or half my pains.

No, I can't tell all my distress
    Or half my pains.

THE NOTHING SONG

Sheer nothing's all I'm singing of:
Not me and no one else, of course;
There's not one word of youth and love
    Nor anything;
I thought this up, once, on my horse
    While slumbering.

I don't know my own sign at birth;
I'm neither native here nor strange;
I don't feel gloom, I don't feel mirth.
    Don't blame me, though—
One night a fairy worked this change
    That's made me so.

I don't know if I sleep or wake
Unless somebody's told me that.
This heart of mine is sure to break
    For grief and care,
Yet the whole thing's not worth one sprat
    To me, I swear.

I'm sick and shivering with death-fright
Though all I know is what I've heard.
I'll seek the doctor who seems right—
    Who is he, though?
He's a great doctor if I'm cured;
    If worse, not so.

My little friend (I don't know who
Since she's a girl I've never seen)
Gives me no grief or joy—that's true,
    Which suits me fine;
No French—or Norman's come between
    Housewalls of mine.

Guilhem IX of Poitiers

Though I've not seen her, my love's strong;
Not seeing her, I'm not undone;
She never did me right or wrong
     And who cares, for
I know a nicer, fairer one
     Worth plenty more.

As for her homeland, I don't know
Whether she's from the hills or plain;
I don't dare claim she's wronged me so
     I can't help grieve;
Yet staying here is such a pain
     I'm going to leave.

Marcabrun (Troubadour)

THE PEASANT LASSIE

Near a hedgerow, sometime recent,
There I met a shepherd lassie
Full of mother wit and sassy,
Some good peasant woman's lassie.
She wore shoes and woolen socks, too,
Blouse and skirt and linen smock, too,
All homespun, quite coarse but decent.

Toward her, through the fields I started;
"Lass," says I, "though you're so pretty,
Chill winds nip you, more's the pity."
"Master," says this peasant lassie,
"Thanks be to God and my good nurse, now,
Winds can blow—I'm none the worse, now,
Since I'm healthy and light-hearted."

"Lass," says I, "you're sweet and girlish;
I turned off the highroad only
So you wouldn't be so lonely.
Such an innocent young lassie
Shouldn't go out unbefriended
Keeping all these sheepflocks tended
In a land so rough and churlish."

"Sir," says she, "though you can take me
How you like, I know what's senseless.
Take your friendship for the friendless,
Master," says this peasant lassie,
"And please put it someplace fitting.
Girls like me can think they're getting
What they want; they'll find it's fakery."

Marcabrun

"Lass, but you're high-born, not common;
Surely some knight was your father
Or he couldn't give your mother
Such a well-bred peasant lassie.
While I watch, you grow more lovely;
Joy would get the better of me
If you'd only be more human."

"Sir, I'll take an oath by heaven
All my family's bloodlines trickle
Straight back to the plow and sickle.
Master," says this peasant lassie,
"Some folks play at being knightly
Who should do such hard work rightly
Six days out of every seven."

"Lass, some fairy queen must love you,
For at your birth she bewitched you
With a beauty that enriched you
More than any peasant lassie;
Yet you'd seem just twice the wonder
If, once, I could get you under
While I was the one above you."

"Sir, plain folks will think it's shocking
Hearing me so overrated;
Don't make my price so inflated,
Master," says this peasant lassie.
"Or here's how you'll get rewarded:
Clear out. Don't stand there, retarded,
In the noonday sunshine, gawking."

"Lass, such wild hearts, fiercely beating,
Gentle down with time and using.
I can see, on slight perusing,
One could offer some young lassie
A most valuable connection,

If his heart's filled with affection,
And if they don't start in cheating."

"Sir, a man whose brain's gone balmy
Swears great oaths, but he's still crazy.
Why make vows and try to praise me?
Master," says this peasant lassie,
"At your price I feel no urging
To sell my state as a virgin
For the whore that folks would call me."

"Lass, each bird and beast, each dumb thing
Always turns back to its nature.
Side by side, creature to creature,
Let us go down, little lassie,
Through the meadowlands together;
There in safety and deep heather
We'll try out our own sweet something."

"Sir, that's true; it follows justly
Madmen will make mad advances;
Courtiers choose the court's romances;
Peasants take a peasant lassie.
Men who've got no good proportion
Bring good sense straight to abortion—
All the ancients warn us, thusly."

"Lass, I never met a lassie
With a face so fair and sassy
And a heart so cold and cruel."

"Sir, the owl gives you this saying:
By an image one man's praying
While one gawks there like a fool."

Jaufre Rudel (Troubadour)

A FAR-OFF LOVE

When days grow long and warm with May,
Then birds' sweet sounds re-echo far;
While exiled long and far away
I call to mind my love afar.
    Bent to eclipse in dark desire,
    No sweet bird's song, no flowering briar
    Content me more than winter's chill.

My lord keeps faith, so I believe
That I shall see my love afar;
Though for each joy that I receive
I gain two griefs since she's so far.
    Ay! might I keep that vow of mine,
    I'd go a pilgrim to that shrine
    Where her bright eyes shine lovely still.

By God's own love, what joys must be
Within love's citadel afar.
Should she consent, I'd lodge nearby
Who now must lie alone afar.
    Never on earth shall speech seem dear
    As when this far-off love comes near
    To tell love's news and take its fill.

To leave her must seem sad and sweet
When once I've met my love afar,
Yet if we'll ever come to meet
I know not since she dwells so far.
    Such tracks and trails, such land and sea,
    Lie still between my love and me,
    Though all things lie in God's good will.

No joy in love shall e'er be mine
Until I see my love afar;
Above all worth her beauties shine,
Above all others, near and far.
  Gladly I'd lie at her command,
  A captive in some Moorish land
  Her precious bidding to fulfill.

Dear Lord, who formed this world entire,
Who shaped for me my love afar,
Pray grant that power I most desire,
To witness soon my love afar.
  Where I shall meet that glorious face,
  In chamber or in garden place,
  That spot shall be my palace still.

That man speaks true who'd say I burn
For naught else than my love afar;
Now toward no other end I yearn—
Only to know my love afar.
  Yet as my fates lie still athwart,
  A curse fall on my godsire's heart
  Who's cursed me so my love runs ill.

Bernart de Ventadorn (Troubadour)

NOW WHEN I SEE THE LARK UPLIFT

Now when I see the lark uplift
His wings for joy in dawn's first ray
Then lets himself, oblivious, drift
For all his heart is glad and gay,
Ay! such great envies seize my thought
To see what raptures others find,
I marvel that desire does not
Consume away this heart of mine.

Alas, I thought I'd grown so wise;
How much in love I had to learn:
I can't prevent this heart that flies
To her who pays love no return.
Ay! now she steals, through love's worst theft,
My heart, my self, my world entire;
She steals herself and I am left
Only this longing and desire.

Lost all control, I've lost all right
To rule my life; my life's her prize
Since first she showed me true delight
In those bright mirrors, her two eyes.
Ay! once I'd caught myself inside
Her glances, I've been drowned in sighs,
Dying as fair Narcissus died
Where streams reflect their captive skies.

Deep in despair, I'll place no trust
In women, though I did before;
I've been their guardian so it's just
That I renounce them evermore;
When none will lift me from my fall,
Since she has cast me down in shame,
Now I distrust them, one and all,
I've learned too well they're all the same.

She acts as any woman would—
Small wonder I'm dissatisfied;
She'll never do the things she should;
She only wants what's been denied.
Ay! now I fall in deep disgrace,
A fool upon love's bridge am I;
No one knows how this could take place
Unless I dared to climb too high.

All mercy's gone, all pity lost—
Though at the best I still knew none—
Since she who should have mercy most
Shows me the least of anyone.
Wrongful it seems now, in my view,
Knowing this creature Love's betrayed
Who'd seek no other good than you,
Then let him die without your aid.

Since she, my Lady, shows no care
To earn my thanks nor pays Love's rights;
Since she'll not hear my constant prayer
And my love yields her no delights,
I say no more; I silent go.
She gives me death; let death reply.
My Lady will not hold me so
I leave, exiled to pain for aye.

Tristan, you'll hear no more from me:
I leave to wander, none knows where;
Henceforth all lovers' joys I flee
And all my songs I now forswear.

Raimbaut d'Aurenga (Troubadour)

BEG PARDON, LORDS

Beg pardon, Lords, but who knows what
Kind of a song this is I'll sing?
Vers? *Sirventes*? Or *estribot*?
What do you call this sort of thing?
How can you say what's right or not?
How can I end this, warranting
    nobody ever saw one like it, made by man or by
    woman, in this whole century or the one just past?

You'll try to tell me I'm insane
But that won't make me break my vow
To speak my feelings clear and plain.
Don't blame me if I can't see how
This wide world could be worth one grain
Compared to things I see right now.
    I'll tell you why, too: if I started this thing and couldn't
    bring it off, you'd think I'm an idiot. I'd rather have six
    cents in hand then a thousand suns in the sky.

No friends of mine need ever fear
They'll anger me by things they've done.
If they can't help me, then and there,
They can relieve me later on.
Still, she defeats and cheats me here
More readily than anyone—
    I say all this because of a lady who keeps me hanging
    on, with sweet talk and lots of waiting. My Lords, can
    she do me any good?

It's been a full four months or more—
Yes, but a thousand years seems less—
Since she gave in to me and swore
She'd give what I long to possess.
My heart's your prisoner; therefore,
Lady, sweeten my bitterness.
    God help me! *In nomine patri et filii et spiritus sancti!*
    Lady, what's coming off?

You make me rage, make me cavort;
You make me write songs fierce with glee.
I've left three ladies of a sort
Who had no peer but you, Lady.
For these mad love songs through the court
Crooner's the name they're calling me.
    Lady, do just anything you please with me, like Lady
    Emma with the shoulder bone—she stuck it in just any-
    place it pleased her.

Here's where I'll end my *what's-its-name*
Since that's the name I've just devised;
No other song sounds much the same
So that's the term I'll utilize.
You'll like it best if you declaim
The whole thing once it's memorized.
    And if anyone ever asks you who made this thing, just
    say it's a man who knows how to do a lot of things,
    and does them right any time he wants to.

Heinrich von Morungen (Minnesinger)

THEN DAYLIGHT CAME

Alas, shall I no longer see,
Glimmering through the night,
Whiter than snow could be,
Her body clear and bright
Till that illus'ry gleam
Grew in my eyes to seem
The radiant moon's beam.
Then daylight came.

"Alas, will he no longer stay
Until the broad day's dawning?
May our nights pass away
So we've no cause for mourning,
'Alas, now comes the day,'
As sorrowing he would say
When by me last he lay.
Then daylight came."

Alas, the way she never stopped
Kissing me in my sleep
Until at last she dropped
Those tears she could not keep;
I brought her comfort then;
She left off weeping when
She wrapped me close again.
Then daylight came.

"Alas, how many times he lost
Himself in seeing me
And from our bedstead tossed
Our covers off to see
Poor me in nakedness;
It seemed miraculous
He never tired of this.
Then daylight came."

Walter von der Vogelweide (Minnesinger)

UNDER THE LINDEN

Under the linden
On the heather,
There we two made that bed of ours;
Sweet the grass within and
Lain together
With newly gathered meadow flowers.
Near the woodland, down the dale,
Tandaradei!
Sweetly sang the nightingale.

I came to meet him
Yet already
Found my true love waiting there before.
Then I heard a greeting
(Gentle Lady!)
Fills me with pleasure evermore.
Did he kiss me? All too well.
Tandaradei!
Look how red my lips still swell.

There my love had woven
Only for me
Our bed of flowers, richly laid.
Should a man go roving,
He'd smile warmly
If he came beneath the linden's shade;
There he'd see, in roses red,
Tandaradei!
Where I'd cradled, soft, my head.

   That he lay beside me,
May they never
Learn that and shame me; God forbid!
Now whate'er betide me
No one ever,
Just he and I know what we did—
One besides, one tiny bird;
       Tandaradei!
He's too true to tell a word.

       — translated with Rosmarie Waldrop

Meister Alexander (Minnesinger)

YEARS LONG GONE

Years long gone, we children playing
Roamed the fields and meadows straying
Through the springtime of our days;
There we ran our careless ways,
     Sometimes violets finding,
       Garlands winding
Where we now see cattle graze.

Now we call to mind those hours
When we sat among the flowers
And the loveliest one we chose.
Then we knew all childhood knows;
     New-made wreaths enhancing
       All our dancing;
So it is the season goes.

Gathering berries would we wander
From the pines to beech trees yonder,
Over stock and over stone,
All the while our bright sun shone;
     Through the woods, the ranger
       Warned of danger
Calling, "Children, get you home."

There, no child too young to carry
Bloodstains of the wild strawberry—
It was only children's play.
Still, we'd heard the shepherd say,
     "Children, take good care now;
       Everywhere now
Snakes lie waiting for their prey."

Through tall weeds a child ran playing
Till he ran back frightened, saying,
"In the grass a snake lay hidden;
Now our playmate has been bitten.
  He cannot recover;
    He must suffer
And be ever sorrow-ridden."

Don't you know how five young maidens
Roamed the meadowlands they strayed in
Till the king had locked his hall?
Sick in shame, they weep and call
  While his jailers grip them
    Fierce and strip them
To the bare flesh, one and all.

Wizlaw von Rügen (Minnesinger)

DARK LEAVES ARE FLYING

Dark leaves are flying
From the trees down through the glen;
Branches stand forsaken.
Shriveled and drying
Stand the flowers, so lovely when
In their day they waken.
  Now frost must send under
  Every growing thing and green,
  And must plunge my thoughts far in sorrow.
  Searching, I wander;
  Though the winter blows so keen,
  Surely new pleasures spring tomorrow.

Give my song powers
For some thousand pleasures, all
Beyond Maytime's bringing:
Roses in showers
From my lady's cheeks do fall—
Such joys be my singing.
  Then let frost oppress me;
  Those sweet scents I would enjoy
  Still are found among all her treasures.
  Should her love bless me,
  My beloved brings such joy
  I could covet no lesser pleasures.

Oswald von Wolkenstein (Minnesinger)

THERE CAME A TIME

I.

There came a time, I was no more than ten years old,
I had to find what mysteries this world might hold;
In many a cranny, starved and wretched, scorched or cold,
   I made my bed by Christians, Greeks and heathen.
Three pennies in my pocket and one dry bread crust,
I left my home to follow friends no man should trust;
Since then, I've spilled so much red blood in foreign dust,
   Sometimes I hoped I'd had my last day's breathing.

      On foot I ran,
      A sorry man
        Too poor to ride;
      Fourteen years passed
      But then at last
        My father died.
      I stole a gray
      Mule foal one day
        To soothe my pride;
But soon I lost him and I felt it bad, then.
      Post, groom or cook—
      I gladly took
        What work was there;
      Off Crete, what's more,
      I pulled an oar
        Or had to steer.
      I found enough
      Things could get rough
        There and elsewhere;
A plain coarse jacket was the best I had, then.

Oswald von Wolkenstein

II.

Through Prussia, Latvia, Turkey, Tartary overseas,
With two kings' troops through France and Spain and Lombardy,
My own heart drove me on and I paid my own fees;
   Reuprecht and Sigmund came with eagle banners.
In French, Castilian, Moorish, I could get along—
Wend, Russian, Latin, Lombard and the Norman tongue.
I played the drum and fiddle or I piped and sung.
   I used ten languages and strange men's manners.

      My way revealed
      Both isle and field
         Where strange flags waved.
      In many a boat
      I kept afloat
         When high winds raved.
      On many a sea
      Storms threatened me
         Yet was I saved.
The Black Sea taught me how to clutch a barrel.
      Mast, sail and plank,
      My whole ship sank
         From under me;
      As merchantman,
      My luck still ran
         To rescue me.
      A Russian, too,
      Fought his way through
         That boiling sea.
My cargo sank, yet I swam free from peril.

III.

The Queen of Aragon was delicate and sweet.
I stretched my beard out to her, kneeling at her feet;
With slim white hands, she wound a little ring there, neat,
    And said, "This tie be never disentangled!"
Then in her fingers took a brazen needle, thin,
And swiftly pierced my earlobes, stabbing through the skin;
As is their custom, she fixed two gold rings therein
    And long I wore the things—you call them bangles.

        I hunted 'round
        Until I found
          Sigmund our king.
        He gave a start
        And crossed his heart
          At our meeting;
        Still, knowing me,
        He called, "Let's see
          This trifling thing."
And friendly asked, "You're not hurt by the ring, then?"
        Women and men,
        They all came then
          To laugh and stare.
        At Perpignan
        Some nine kings' men
          Were there that year.
        Their Pope, whose name
        Was Pedro, came
          From Luna there
With those from Prado and the Romish king, then.

Oswald von Wolkenstein

IV.

I tried to change this stupid life, I must confess;
I was some kind of monk for two whole years, no less.
I know this started in my great devotedness,
    Yet love could bring it all to ruins, finally.
Soon, off to tournaments and knighthood games I swept,
There to perform that lady's will with whom I slept,
Yet had I not still worn that monk's hood that I kept,
    She would have treated any dolt as kindly.

        A little while
        My fates would smile
          And pamper me
        While the wool flap
        Of my monk's cap
          Still snuggled me;
        I've had no girl
        Could cling and curl
          So lovingly,
Heard all I said and gave so little trouble.
        Still, soon enough
        This holy love
          Had shot its load;
        I flung my hood
        Off in the wood
          And took the road.
        Now work and strife
        Reign in this life
          Where joy once flowed.
Now every joy is half, but pain goes double.

V.

To count my troubles through would surely take too long;
In all this world, just one red mouth could loose my tongue.
My heart is wounded, hurt to death with bitter wrong.
  Because of her, my sweat ran down in rivers.
I flushed and paled; I panted like one heavy laden,
Yet I fulfilled each service for this gentle maiden.
I sometimes felt the senses of this body fading;
  As if I burned, I turned all sighs and shivers.

         I made my way
         Both night and day
           Two hundred mile;
         So sore distressed
         I found no rest
           In all that while.
         Cold, rain and snow
         Could bring me no
           Such bitter trial;
I melt as frost melts when her dear sun warms me.
         Yet should I sleep
         With her, I'd keep
           My slavery;
         I plow a street
         Of rocks, complete
           With misery—
         Raging and wild
         Till mercy mild
           Bends her to me
Since only she could change this grief that harms me.

Oswald von Wolkenstein

VI.

I have endured now more than 37 years
Of madness, raging, song and poetry and tears;
High time I settled down like any man who hears
   No cries, but something in its cradle calling.
Yet her I nevermore forget who brought to birth
This foolish rage of heart that drove me through the earth,
Though nowhere could I find one equal to her worth.
   Besides, I can't help fear a wife's tongue, bawling.

      Last, I'll relate
      The wise and great
        Have valued me;
      They'd heard my tongue
      Spin out its song
        Delightedly.
      I'm Wolkenstein:
      This life of mine
        Goes senselessly—
For this vile earth, I've kept too much desire.
      Yet I know well
      No man can tell
        His day to die;
      We take along
      No work nor song
        To help us by.
      Had I seen cause
      To keep the laws
        Of God on high,
I'd have less cause to fear His storms of fire.

       —translated with William MacDonald

Anonymous, French Pavane

LADY WHO LOCKS MY SOUL

Lady who locks my soul in
    This capture of your eyes,
Whose gracious smile has stolen
    My spirit for your prize,
Grant some reprieve or I
Must surely pine and die.

Dear one, why must you leave me
    When I am near at hand?
Your lovely eyes bereave me
    Of sense and self-command;
Your pure perfections sway
My actions, night and day.

Through heavenly discourses,
    Through loveliness and charm,
You ravish all my forces
    And work this heart much harm,
Touching my life to fire
With love and love's desire.

Spared from a lover's passion
    My heart went fancy-free;
Now love takes full possession
    Of my desires and me;
Love's law obtains through both
My spirit and my troth.

Come nearer then, my beauty,
    Come nearer still, my own;
No more evade love's duty;
    My heart is yours alone.
Now with a single kiss
Change all love's pain to bliss.

Anonymous

Angel, I here surrender
   To die within your kiss;
Those lips so soft and tender
   Have rapt my soul in this;
In love's encounter, all
My spirits headlong fall.

Sooner the tides of ocean
   Shall turn and surge uphill,
Earth's sun forswear his motion
   And leave this world to chill
Before this love of mine
Subsides or knows decline.

—translated with Françoise Roulet

Jehan Plançon

WET WITH DEWS

When the green fields lighted o'er
  With the dawning of the day,
By her side whom I adore
  I went to the woods to play.
      Wet with dews of the pretty month of May,
    My true love beside me lay.

There where flowers flourish around
  And some thousand songbirds sing,
To the rushing water's sound
  I told my heart's sorrowing.
    Wet with dews . . .

While I held her close and clasped her
  She'd embrace me and entwine
So that to the wall no faster
  Clings the climbing ivy vine.
    Wet with dews . . .

Playfully I pressed and pecked her
  Perky bosom half-undressed;
There my sweet tooth plucked pure nectar:
  Wild strawberries of her breast.
    Wet with dews . . .

"Oh my dear love," then said she,
  " You've gone far too far I fear."
Still she kissed and clung to me
  While she nibbled at my ear.
    Wet with dews . . .

Jehan Plançon

Then I whispered, growing bolder,
   Though I daren't breathe a word
Of the secret things I told her;
   You'd hear too well what you heard.
      Wet with dews . . .

There's no land, no empery
   I'd exchange this true love for;
Such the joys it brings to me
   Saying now and evermore:
      Wet with dews of the pretty month of May,
      My true love beside me lay.

Jean Baptiste Besard

SUCH SORROWS LIE IN LOVING THEE

Such sorrows lie in loving thee
   Whose state of heart forever changeth,
Shifting more restless than the sea
   That to no vantage ever rangeth.
      What use to love but thee alone?
      All favor lies in thee unknown.
      Now shall I never find content;
      Now I forever all repent.

Yet let us still dispute for aye;
   Let each display his full resources;
Thy frenzied loves I vow to buy
   And free thee from unfaithful forces.
      Then shalt thou yield in turn to me
      Thy reason and thy liberty.
      Now shall I never find content;
      Now I forever all repent.

Yield up this heart, no longer mine;
   Yield up that source of all thy beauties;
If not yield that, yield naught of thine;
   To be thyself exceeds all duties.
      As this my song exceeds in lies,
      So light, so faithless prove thine eyes.
      Now shall I never find content;
      Now I forever all repent.

Gabriel Bataille

WHO WANTS TO CURE A MIGRAINE

Who wants to cure a migraine, let him
Drink up good wine and scuppernong,
Sausage and ham at table set him
And keep his pantry freshly hung.
  Water's no good; it only rots your lung.
   Down it, down it, down it; flood it down your tongue;
  Drain it off, good lads, we'll brim it from the bung.

Wine that's beloved by our good father,
Keeping him handsome, lithe and young,
Makes us so wise we never bother
Studying, since we're never wrong.
  Water's no good; . . .

Old father Lot, once drunk in a cavern,
Got his own daughters great with young,
Proving elixirs bought in a tavern
Pass every doctor's cures headlong.
  Water's no good; . . .

Drain off your glass; let every kidney
Flow with a function fresh and strong.
Death to the man so vile and piddly
He'd slander those he drinks among.
  Water's no good; it only rots your lung.
   Down it, down it, down it; flood it down your tongue;
  Drain it off, good lads, we'll brim it from the bung.

Girolamo Frescobaldi

WHILE SOFTER BREEZES ALL SIGH

While softer breezes all sigh, beguiling,
   Youthfully smiling
      Unfolds the rose;

Unseared by summer, with cool bravado,
   In emerald shadow
      The green hedge glows.

Lightly, come lightly, come dance youth's measure,
   Nymphs, while your treasure
      Of beauty grows,

While every crystal wandering fountain
   From highest mountain
      To ocean flows,

While every bird his sweet aria's singing,
   Each shrub new-springing,
      Each blossom blows—

Now from the shadows, let one face, pretty,
   Smile to show pity
      That ends love's woes.

Lightly, nymphs, lightly, carol together;
   Calm that harsh weather
      Love's scorn bestows.

Anonymous, *Cancionero Musical de Palacio*

DO IT SO IT'S DONE

> *Do it so it's done,*
> *You West Virginia virgin.*
> *Do it so it's done;*
> *They've called me home—it's urgent.*

There's a girl down in Carolina; (*bis*)
She let me take a look at her veg-
   etable garden she'd been weeding.
> *Do it so it's done . . .*

There's a girl, just as sweet as honey; (*bis*)
She let me take a look at her cun-
   ning loaf of bread she was kneading.
> *Do it so it's done . . .*

There's a girl and her name was Alice; (*bis*)
She let me take a look at her fal-
   con she was carefully feeding.
> *Do it so it's done . . .*

She's a virgin, that's the rumor; (*bis*)
Still, no one doubts her claim to scru-
   ples and the very best form of breeding.
> *Do it so it's done . . .*

She kept wanting to have some dinner; (*bis*)
But first I wanted to get in-
   spired by that good book she was reading.

>   *Do it so it's done,*
> *You West Virginia virgin.*
>   *Do it so it's done;*
> *They've called me home—it's urgent.*

—translated with Jaime Ferran

Tinodi Sebestyén

ALL SORTS OF DRUNKARDS

Hearken, all you drunkards, while I sing your wickedness,
All the sins committed in your raging drunkenness;
Time and time again forgetting all God's righteousness.

Let's begin when Father Noah climbed down from the Ark,
Letting all his animals and people disembark;
Then God bade them multiply, go out and make their mark.

Down there came a billy goat that stumbled on a vine,
Gobbled up a grape that filled him with a spark divine,
Frisked around the place and shook his whiskers, long and fine.

Noah, when he heard of that, went straightway out and got
Vines to plant behind his house and start a garden spot.
Then he ordered blood of goats and monkeys should be brought.

Next, he ordered blood of lions, then the blood of swine;
Using all that beastly blood, he watered down the vine;
When the grapes grew plump, he filled his barrels with good wine.

Soon as Noah sampled that, he fell down stinking drunk,
Fell asleep, incontinently, naked on his bunk;
Ham, his son, laughed right out loud to see his naked trunk.

All young men and women, learn a lesson from the texts:
To your drunken parents you must pay your full respects;
Otherwise you'll have to bear their curses on your necks.

Listen now, you drunkards, you must grasp the liquor laws:
Men have different traits and different wines must be the cause.
Some partake of lion's blood till roaring fills their jaws.

They grow brave as Samson, stout in courage, filled with might;
They don't think a thing of daring champions to fight;
Sobered up, they'll creep behind the bushes, out of sight.

Any ape is filled with pranks and dodges, through and through,
Imitating cleverly what other creatures do;
Some who share his blood take part in monkey business, too.

Any pig's a vile, disgusting thing of trash and crud;
Little caring for his coat, he wallows in the mud;
So do all the drunkards who partake of swinish blood.

Men who share the blood of goats are all too often found;
Growing rank and goatish, they will rant or leap and bound;
Some butt heads like rams while others buckjump all around.

There's a kind of peaceful drunk whose head is humbly bowed;
Second, there's the thug that gets obstreperous, rough and proud;
Third, the weepy drunk that prays and counts his sins out loud;

Fourth, the sort of drunk who covets anything he's shown;
Fifth, the kind that steals and carts off everything you own;
Sixth, the drunk that sits there silent, stupid as a stone;

Seventh, comes the drunk that grows as wise as Damian's steed,
Argues high theology, expounds the Prophet's Creed;
Once he's sober, hand the man a text—the fool can't read!

Eighth, you've met the kind of drunk that hangs around the court;
Neither wise nor brave, he has no skill of any sort;
He knows how to flatter, though, and sell your honor short.

Some men get so drunk they just can't find the bridge at all;
Crossing underneath in muck and slime, they slip and sprawl;
None but beasts, you'd think, would get down on all fours
            to crawl.

Tinodi Sebestyén

Some have filthy faces; some have hairdos just like mops;
One flops in your kitchen or else down your cellar drops;
On your choicest vintages they clown and spin like tops.

Pretty girls and women must behave themselves just right;
At the meals they serve you, they won't touch a single bite;
When they're by themselves, whole roasted capons pass from
        sight.

When, beside the window sill, they sit embroidering lace,
Girls pull out a tiny flask they've hidden some dark place;
After every stitch or two, they'll try a little taste.

Never far behind them come the ancient crones and hags;
All the wine they get they hide in cedar chests or bags;
Young girls find and steal it; then, oh how the old tongue wags!

Wines are scorned by all wet nurses with enormous jugs;
Still, they'll taste it, just to help the milk inside their dugs;
Next, they fall down drunk and squash their babies flat as bugs.

Come now, all you drunkards grown so riotous and bold,
Think on all these sins against the Lord that I've just told.
End this drunken life. Reform. Come back into the fold.

God the Lord created wine to serve a noble aim;
Temp'rately he lets us drink it down and that's no shame;
Thus the whole wide world may see some cause to praise His
        name.

Now let's drink our wine up with firm hearts and full accord;
Still, we'd never sin against our country and our Lord;
All transgressors of this law, damnation's your reward!

Tinodi Sebestyén

One they call Sebestyén wrote this song in bitter thirst;
In Nyirbator, 1548, he sang it first;
Stewards of the Court, now give us wine or stand accursed!

Søren Terkelsen

HYLAS PROPOSES TO NOT GET MARRIED

What could coax me into marriage?—
      You get headaches then go broke!
First it's servants, then a carriage;
      Women are the strangest folk.
If she's rich, she'll be the master;
      If she's poor, who'll buy the bread?
Young, she'd tempt men toward disaster;
      Old, I'd just as soon be dead.

Money's poured out for a wedding—
      Costly outfits must be worn;
Next, that baby you've been dreading
      Might develop and get born.
Nursemaids want the choicest victual,
      Plump themselves on meat and stout;
Better think on this a little
      Or your child might do without.

Aren't boxes, brooms and barrels,
      Chests and armchairs mighty dear?—
Shitty Kate's, the cook's, apparel,
      All her kitchen tools and gear:
Glasses, dishclothes, then a table,
      Jugs and mugs and plates enough—
Who in all creation's able
      To afford such piles of stuff?

Many mouths are yours to nourish;
      There's a famished dog and cat.
Guests might come—they'd think it boorish
      Just to turn them out like that.
Meat and fish cost lots of money;
      Beer and bread and wine are worse;
What your platters serve a-plenty
      Quickly empties out your purse.

Then the wife will start in clamoring—
      Always wanting to be boss;
Like as not, she'll get a hammering
      Since that makes a husband cross.
Then whenever friends come calling
      She'll complain and curse her lot.
Folks will say her life's appalling;
      That could put him on the spot.

Many a man, from wedlock's trenches,
      Flees his house and spouse to roam,
Takes to drinking, cards or wenches;
      Day and night he won't go home
While the wife from whom he's wandered
      Hasn't one crust to her name;
All they owned he's quickly squandered,
      So his children live in shame.

As for me, I'm sure I'd never
      Want to cause such storm and strife;
I'll go on the same as ever—
      Lots of women in my life:
One today, the next tomorrow;
      That's my key to mental health
And the antidote to sorrow:
      Each one looks out for himself.

Franz Schubert and Johann Müller

THE ORGAN GRINDER

Out beyond the village stands an organ man
And with numb, stiff fingers plays the best he can;

On the ice he falters barefoot, here and there,
And his little platter stays forever bare.

No one seems to listen, no one seems to care
How the hounds go snarling 'round the old man there.

And he lets it happen—all goes as it will—
Turns his hurdy-gurdy that is never still.

Strange old man, shall I then go with you along?
On your hurdy-gurdy will you play my song?

Gustav Mahler

IN PRAISE OF REASON

It happened in a leafy vale,
Cuckoo and nightingale
     Wagered to end their quarrel
By singing for the master part,
To win by luck or win by art—
     The winner wear the laurel.

The cuckoo said, "If you'll permit,
I'll pick a judge that's fit,"
     Deciding for a donkey directly—
"Because he owns two lofty ears,
     Lofty ears, lofty ears,
And knows the best of what he hears,
     He can judge correctly!"

So when they came before the bar
He said, "We call this court of law
     To order. Start the singing."
The nightingale sang clear and far.
The ass declared, "He's awfully hard!
     He's awfully hard! He-haw! He-haw!
We don't see what he's thinking!"

But cuckoo set out sure and swift
To sing through Third and Fourth and Fifth.
The ass was pleased but just said, "Halt!
Halt! Halt! Our verdict shall be given.
     Yea, given!

"This nightingale has sung quite well.
Oh but cuckoo, you grand chorale!
     Grand chorale!
     You hold the beat with rigor!
     Sweet rigor!

Gustav Mahler

We speak this from our reasoning mind!
Reasoning mind! Reasoning mind!
Regardless of the cost we find
You are the major figure.
The figure!"

Cuckoo! Cuckoo!
He-haw!

NOTES

I. POEMS

p. 17.   Publius Ovidius Naso (43 B.C.–17 A.D.) from *Metamorphoses, II.*

p. 20.   Antonio Vivaldi (1678–1741), *La Quattro Stagioni.* These sonnets may have been written either by Vivaldi or one of his librettists. In early publications the poems appear intact at the head of the score, but also distributed, phrase by phrase, through the music to show what is depicted at each point. In translation it was necessary to preserve this original order of phrases.

p. 22.   Joseph Freiherr von Eichendorff (1788–1885), "Auf Meines Kindes Tot (8)."

p. 23.   Gerard de Nerval (1808–1885), "El Desdichado" [The Desolate].

p. 24.   "Koz'ma Petrovich Prutkov," "Vianet list, prokhodit leto," "Pamiat' proshlogo," "Cherviak i popad'ia" and "Chestoliubie." This supposed poet, playwright, and epigrammatist was a hoax invented by Count Alexei Tolstoy (1817–1875) and friends.

p. 27.   Mihai Eminescu (1849–1889) was Romania's greatest poet; he deeply influenced the development of the language. His "Sonnet," from a group of three, relates to his long, tormented love affair with Veronica Micle.

p. 31.   Arthur Rimbaud (1854–1891), "Memoire." The poem reflects the traumas of Rimbaud's childhood near Charleville in France, particularly his father's (the sun's) flight from the mother (the river) and his resulting isolation and bitterness.

p. 33.   Christian Morgenstern (1871–1914), the best known German comic poet. "Das Knie," "Die Mausefalle," "Die Kugeln,"

"Palmström an Eine Nachtigall," "Die Behörde," "Die Hecht" and "Tapetenblume."

p. 39. Rainer Maria Rilke (1875–1926). *Sonette an Orpheus*, "Archascher Torso Apollos," "Schlaflied" and "Der Panther." Some of these poems have been published by Houghton Mifflin as translated by A. Poulin, Jr. Dealing with such rich and complex materials, fellow translators do not compete but collaborate.

p. 47. Corrado Govoni (1884–1965), "Paesi." Italian Futurist poet and critic.

p. 31. Federico García Lorca (1889–1936), "Romance Sonámbulo." The best known of Lorca's *Gypsy Ballads* tells of a wounded Gypsy smuggler who returns to find that his lover, despairing, has drowned herself. The opening lines, passed from mouth to mouth, were famous even before publication.

p. 51. Yehuda Amichai (1924–), "Kelev Akherei Ha-ahava." Amichai is the best known living Israeli poet.

p. 52. Leszek Szaruga (1946–), "Licentia Poetica," "Pomiedzy" and "Kolonia Karna." Pseudonym of Alexander Wirpsza, son of a famous Polish poet; he spent much of his career underground with Solidarity working for Polish democracy.

p. 55. Marin Sorescu (1936–1996), "Am Legat . . . ," "Ţaranii," "Hoţii," "Fortareaţa," "O Amœba" and "Dincolo." Recognized as Romania's finest playwright; many also saw him as her best poet. With a strong peasant background, his poems have heavy echoes of folksong and popular myth.

p. 61. Ian Mircea (1947–), "Sibiu în Ceaţa." Poet and editor, living in Sibiu, Romania.

II. FOLK SONGS AND BALLADS

p. 65. French Folk Ballad: "Le Blanche Biche."

p. 68.　Five Hungarian Folk Songs: "A Rossz Feleség," "El kéne indulni,""Kocsi, szekér, kocsi, szán," "Ha kimegyek arr' a magos" and "Altal mennek én a Tiszán." Though not classified as a ballad, "The Bad Wife" has cognates in many European languages.

p. 72.　Two Romanian Folk Ballads: "Miorîta" and "Meşterul Manole." "The Ewe Lamb" is known in some version to almost every Romanian; no cognates are found elsewhere in the European ballad regions. This version was collected by the romantic poet, Alecsandrii. "Master Builder Manole" is only slightly less well known in Romania. Unlike "The Ewe Lamb," cognate songs and ballads (known by type as "The Walled-up Wife") exist throughout Europe; the English version is "London Bridge." This version was also collected by Alecsandrii.

p. 87.　Four Romanian Folk Songs: "Tucu-te iegute plina," "Parinte, sfintia ta," "Saraca mindruca mea" and "Saracii boii cornuti." Songs from the private collection of Dr. Dumitru Pop of Cluj.

p. 89.　Seven German Folk Songs: "In Meines Vaters Garten," "Brüder, wir müssen ziehen in den Krieg," "Es War'n Einmal Neun Schneider," "Was haben wir Gänse für Kleidung an?" "Greiner Zanner, Schnöpfitzer," "Zwischen Berg und Tiefen Thal" and "Es Wolt Ein Meydlein Grassen Gan." The three vulgar street songs were given learned polyphonic settings by such Renaissance composers as Heinrich Isaac and Ludwig Senfl.

p. 94.　Three Swedish Folk Songs: "När som jag var på mitt adertonde år," "Nu äro vi redo att vandra" and "A gäck int' än, du Peder." Songs collected in Dalarna and recorded by Margareta Jonth. The original of the first song has seven stanzas.

III. ART SONGS

p. 99.　Guilhem, IXth Count of Poitier and VIIth Duke of Acquitaine (1071–1127), "Ab la Dolchor," "Farai un Vers, Pos mi Sonelh" and "Farai un Vers, de Dreyt Nien." His are the earliest extant Troubadour lyrics. "A New Song for New Days" suggests, however, an already established tradition of courtly love lyrics, while "The Nothing Song" appears to be a parody of that courtly lyric. Outside any such tradition, "Ladies with Cats" seems a song that a prince might compose for a court of warlike nobles.

p. 105. Marcabrun (fl. 1129–1150), "L'Autrier Jost Una Sebissa." The earliest extant example of a *pastorella* or song in which a knight tries to seduce a peasant girl.

p. 108. Jaufre Rudel (fl. middle 12th century), "Lan Quan li Jorn." Early example of a song praising a distant love.

p. 110. Bernart de Ventadorn (fl. 1150–1180), "Can Vei la Lauzeta." The best known song of the most famous Troubadour, remarkable in specifying envy as motive.

p. 112. Raimbaut d'Aurenga (fl. 1150–1173), "Escotatz, Mas No Say," the earliest example of what we might call a "talking blues" — the end of each stanza breaks down into a spoken prose complaint about the difficulty of making songs, earning a living, or the singer's heartless lover.

p. 114. Heinrich von Morungen (d. 1222), "Owe, Sol Aber Mir." Similar to an *alba* or dawn song of the Troubadours, though more personal and affectionate.

p. 116. Walther von der Vogelweide (c. 1170–1230), "Unter der Linden." The most widely known German lyric.

p. 118. Meister Alexander (late 13th century), "Hie vor do Wir Kinder Wâren." A song of seemingly innocent childhood pleasures and of sadistic punishment.

p. 120. Wizlaw III von Rügen (c. 1268–1325), "Loybere Risen." Unlike the typical Troubadour song of a lovelorn springtime, Wizlaw tells how satisfied love compensates him for autumnal weather.

p. 121. Oswald von Wolkenstein (c. 1377–1445), "Es Fuegt Sich . . ." records, with occasional accuracy, the life of this extraordinary adventurer.

p. 127. Anonymous, French Pavane (16th century), "Belle qui Tient ma Vie."

p. 129. Jehan Plançon (1558–1612), "La Rousée du Joly Mois de May." Five of the original's 14 verses.

p. 131. Jean Baptiste Besard (c. 1567–?), "C'est Malheur Que." The melody of this song is familiar from Respighi's "Suite of Ancient Airs and Dances for the Lute."

p. 132. Gabriel Bataille (1574–1630), "Qui Veut Chasser una Migraine."

p. 133. Girolamo Frescobaldi (1583–1643), "Se l'Aura Spira."

p. 134. Anonymous (c. 1500), from *Cancionero Musical de Palacio*, "Da le si le Das."

p. 136. Tinodi Sebestyén, (fl. c. 1550), "Sokféle Részögösről." The original has 60 verses.

p. 140. Søren Terkelsen (c. 1599–1656.) "Hylas vill Intet Giffte Sig."

p. 142. Franz Schubert's (1797–1828) setting of Johann Müller's "Die Leiermann," the final song of *Die Winterreise.*

p. 143. Gustav Mahler's (1860–1911) setting of "Lob des Hohen Verstands," from the collection of folk poems, *Des Knaben Wunderhorn.*

ACKNOWLEDGMENTS

I want to express my gratitude to the Corporation of Yaddo and the Virginia Center for the Creative Arts for periods in residence during which some of these translations were finished. I am also deeply indebted to co-translators who have given generously of their time and insight. These include Tanya Tolstoy, Ioan and Kitty Popa, Sever Trifu, Neli Ament, Dona Roşu, Luciana Costea, Augustin Maissen, Simona Draghici, Lore Segal, Peter Lengyel, Justyna Kostkowska, Paul Archambault, Radu Lupan, Nicolae Babuts, Rosmarie Waldrop, William MacDonald, François Roulet and Jaime Ferran. It has been a genuine pleasure and an enrichment to be able to work with them.

I am grateful, as well, to the editors of the following journals where some of these translations first appeared: *Agenda, American Poetry Review, The Atlantic, Bottighe Oscura, Columbia, Counter/Measures, The Formalist, From Out of the Salt Mound, Grand Street, Green House, Hudson Review, Listen, Mademoiselle, Maryland Poetry Review, Negative Capability, The New Hungarian Review, New World Writing, The North American Review, The Northwest Review, Odyssey, Poetry, Punto de Contacto, The Quarterly Review of Literature, Ramuri, Romanian Bulletin, Salmagundi, Seneca Review, Southern California Anthology, Steaua, The Syracuse Scholar, Teen Chronicle: The Review, Tribuna Magazin, Tribuna Romaniei, TriQuarterly, Wayne Review, The Western Review.*

ABOUT THE AUTHOR

Responsible for the emergence of American confessional poetry, W. D. Snodgrass won the 1960 Pulitzer Prize for Poetry with his first book, *Heart's Needle*. He saw much of our domestic suffering as occurring against a backdrop of a more universal suffering inherent in the whole of human experience. Snodgrass followed that astonishing work with *After Experience; The Führer Bunker: A Cycle of Poems in Progress* (BOA Editions, 1977), nominated for the National Book Critics Circle Award for Poetry and produced by Wynn Handman for the American Place Theatre; *Each in His Season* (BOA, 1993); and *The Fuehrer Bunker: The Complete Cycle* (BOA, 1995). He lives with wife, critic and translator Kathleen Snodgrass in Erieville, New York, and San Miguel de Allende, Mexico.

BOA EDITIONS, LTD.
NEW AMERICAN TRANSLATIONS SERIES

Vol. 1   *Illuminations*
          Poems by Arthur Rimbaud
          Translated by Bertrand Mathieu with Foreword by Henry Miller

Vol. 2   *Exaltation of Light*
          Poems by Homero Aridjis
          Translated by Eliot Weinberger

Vol. 3   *The Whale and Other Uncollected Translations*
          Richard Wilbur

Vol. 4   *Beings and Things on Their Own*
          Poems by Katerina Anghelaki-Rooke
          Translated by the Author in Collaboration with Jackie Willcox

Vol. 5   *Anne Hébert: Selected Poems*
          Translated by A. Poulin, Jr.

Vol. 6   *Yannis Ritsos: Selected Poems 1938–1988*
          Edited and Translated by Kimon Friar and Kostas Myrsiades

Vol. 7   *The Flowers of Evil and Paris Spleen*
          Poems by Charles Baudelaire
          Translated by William H. Crosby

Vol. 8   *A Season in Hell and Illuminations*
          Poems by Arthur Rimbaud
          Translated by Bertrand Mathieu

Vol. 9   *Day Has No Equal but Night*
          Poems by Anne Hébert
          Translated by A. Poulin, Jr.

Vol. 10   *Songs of the Kisaeng*
          Courtesan Poetry of the Last Korean Dynasty
          Translated by Constantine Contogenis and Wolhee Choe

Vol. 11   *Selected Translations*
          W. D. Snodgrass